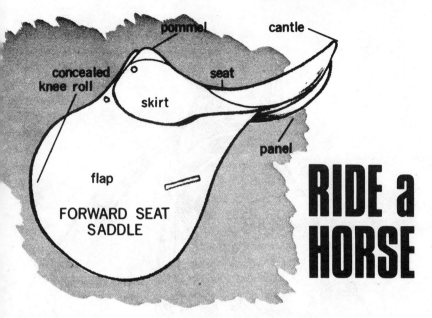

pommel

cantle

concealed
knee roll

seat

skirt

panel

flap

FORWARD SEAT
SADDLE

RIDE a HORSE

Do you want to ride and yet are doubtful about how and where to begin? Do you think that all riding falls into two types – "English" and "Western"? This book by champion horsewoman Jeanne Mellin will tell you about the *three* styles of riding most popular throughout the United States and Canada today, and the appropriate saddles, tack and apparel for each.

Over 100 illustrations by the author supplement her lucid text in providing step-by-step instruction in all three styles of riding, with lively comments and tips on breeds of horses, riding apparel and riding etiquette. More important, the book stresses the need for harmony between horse and rider in the interplay of physical movement and psychological response that is horsemanship.

Author and illustrator of numerous books on horses, Jeanne Mellin lives and works in New York's Dutchess County, on a farm where Morgan horses are bred and trained. A rider since childhood, her studio (where she writes and illustrates her books and does oil paintings of champion horses) bristles with trophies and blue ribbons.

Her approach in this book is forthright, imbued with common sense and the knowledge that comes from experience—she has little patience with show-offs in either Western or English style. If your interest in riding is sincere, this book is for you.

Illustrated Horseback Riding for Beginners

WRITTEN AND ILLUSTRATED

By Jeanne Mellin

Published by
Melvin Powers
WILSHIRE BOOK COMPANY
12015 Sherman Road
No. Hollywood, California 91605
Telephone: (213) 875-1711 / 983-1105

Printed by

HAL LEIGHTON PRINTING COMPANY
P.O. Box 3952
North Hollywood, California 91605
Telephone: (213) 983-1105

Second Printing, 1971

Copyright © 1970 by
Sterling Publishing Co., Inc.
419 Park Avenue South, New York, N.Y. 10016
Simultaneously published and Copyright © 1970 in Canada
by Saunders of Toronto, Ltd., Don Mills, Ontario
Manufactured in the United States of America
Library of Congress Catalog Card No.: 70-90800

ISBN 0-87980-196-4

Contents

GLOSSARY 7

BEFORE YOU BEGIN 11

1. THE THREE SEATS 13
   The Hunt Seat . . . The Stock Seat . . . The Saddle Seat

2. LIGHT HORSE BREEDS.. 20
   The Thoroughbred . . . The Arabian . . . The Anglo-Arab and the
   Half-Bred . . . The Quarter Horse . . . The Morgan Horse . . . The
   American Saddlebred . . . The Tennessee Walking Horse . . . The
   Apaloosa, the Palomino, the Pinto

3. TACK, CLOTHING AND HORSES 26
   Hunt Seat Tack and Outfit . . . Choosing a Horse for the Hunt Seat . . .
   Stock Seat Tack and Outfit . . . Choosing a Stock Horse . . . Saddle
   Seat Tack and Outfit . . . Choosing a Saddle-Type Horse

4. RIDING HUNT SEAT 49
   Bridling the Horse . . . Mounting the Horse . . . Dismounting . . .
   Achieving a Correct Seat . . . The Walk . . . The Trot . . . Posting . . .
   Diagonals . . . The Canter . . . Check Your Progress . . . The Hand
   Gallop . . . Use of Tack . . . A Word about Jumping

5. RIDING STOCK SEAT.. 77
   Bridling . . . Saddling . . . Mounting . . . Achieving a Correct Seat
   . . . The Walk . . . The Jog . . . The Lope . . . Maneuvers at the Lope . . . A
   Few Tips

6. RIDING SADDLE SEAT 98
   Bridling . . . Saddling . . . Mounting . . . Achieving a Correct Seat . . .
   The Walk . . . The Trot . . . Posting . . . Diagonals . . . The Canter . . .
   The Slow Gait and the Rack . . . Using the Show Bridle . . Trotting with
   the Show Bridle . . . Cantering with the Show Bridle

7. A FINAL WORD.. 126

INDEX 127

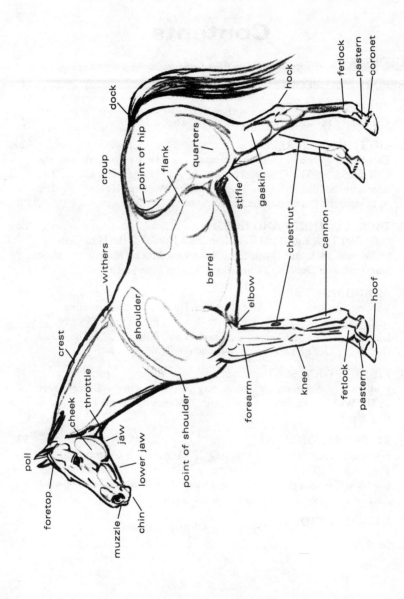

Glossary

Age.	Horses are fully mature at 7 years of age and often live beyond 30. An "aged" horse is one of 9 years or more.
Aids.	The cues or signals given to a horse to make him perform in a certain way. They may be given by the voice, legs, reins, or by shifts in the rider's weight.
Apaloosa.	Often spelled Appaloosa.
Balance.	Balance is not a problem for a riderless horse. As soon as a rider is placed on his back, the horse's center of balance is displaced. Hence the importance of the rider's seat and of collecting the horse.
Billets.	In saddlery, straps which enter a buckle, or loops which receive the end of a buckled strap.
Bit.	The part of the bridle that the horse holds in his mouth.
Bridle.	The apparatus on a horse's head, by which he is controlled.
Canter.	A gait which is, in effect, a controlled or collected gallop.
Cantle.	The raised hind part of a saddle.
Cavesson.	A nose band.
Chunk.	A smallish, but strong and heavily built horse. Originally a small western draft horse suitable as a mount for an over-sized rider.
Cinches.	Double girths attached to a western saddle.
Collect.	To collect a horse is to cause him to bring his entire body into balance, ready to assume any gait or move in any direction desired by the rider.
Colt.	A male horse up to the age of 4.
Croup.	The area of a horse's back behind the saddle.
Curb.	A strap or chain attached to the bit, for restraining the horse.
Dam.	The female horse, or mare, is styled a dam in relation to her offspring.
Equitation.	The art of riding on horseback.
Fender.	The broad leather shield connecting the stirrup with the western saddle.

7

Filly.	A female horse up to the age of 4.
Fine Harness.	Saddlebred Horses are classed as Fine Harness when they are shown drawing a four-wheeled wagon.
Foal.	A new-born horse of either sex.
Gait.	The foot movement naturally employed by a horse at different speeds—walk, trot, canter, gallop and their variations. Also the artificial gaits—pace, rack and slow-gait—in which some horses are schooled by their trainers.
Gaited horse.	A horse which has been trained in the artificial, or man-made, gaits—in other words, a five-gaited horse.
Gallop.	The fastest (about 12 to 35 miles per hour) of the natural gaits, in which the horse goes by leaps and bounds.
Gelding.	A castrated male horse.
Girth.	The belly-band of a saddle.
Grade horse.	A horse one of whose parents is purebred and the other of mixed breed.
Hack.	A horse used for purely recreational riding rather than for hunting, work, showing, etc.
Hacking.	Pleasure riding.
Hand.	A unit of 4 inches, supposedly equal to a hand's breadth, used in measuring the height of horses, from withers to ground.
Hands.	"Good hands" are those of a rider who maintains a constant, light, flexible contact with the horse's mouth.
Head shy.	Describes a horse with the bad habit of throwing his head up to avoid being bridled.
Hock.	The joint midway on the hind leg of a horse (or other quadruped).
Hunter.	A horse, either Thoroughbred, or part-Thoroughbred, used originally for hunting.
Hunter hack.	A horse rated on his ability as both a hunter and a hack.
Irons.	The metal parts of the stirrups.
Jig.	A series of fretful, bouncy steps taken by a nervous or irritated horse.
Jog.	The term applied in western riding to the natural medium gait of the stock horse.

Jumper.	A horse of any breed judged solely on the basis of his ability to jump obstacles.
Light horse breeds.	Breeds suitable for riding, as opposed to heavy breeds, such as draft horses.
Lope.	The term applied in western riding to the natural fast gait of the stock horse.
Manners.	A well-mannered horse is one free of bad habits, obedient and responsive.
Martingale.	A strap passing between the forelegs of a horse, connecting the girth with the bit, intended to keep the horse's head down and thus inhibit him from rearing.
Near side.	The left side of a horse.
Neck-reining.	A well-trained horse will turn when the reins are simply pressed against the side of his neck opposite to the turn.
Off side.	The right side of a horse.
Pacer.	A horse whose manner of stepping is a pace; that is, a gait in which the legs on the same side are lifted together.
Park horse.	A horse with comfortable gaits, good manners and stylish appearance.
Pommel.	The high part of the front of a saddle.
Port.	Part of the bit curved to fit the tongue.
Posting.	The act of alternately rising from the saddle and sinking into it, in rhythm with the horse's movement at the trot.
Purebred.	Describes a horse of unmixed breed; not to be confused with Thoroughbred, which is the name of a particular breed.
Rack.	A man-made gait, in which each foot hits the ground separately.
Registry.	Each breed of horse is represented by an association of breeders who keep pedigrees and other records of horses registered with them. Ancestry is not the sole determinant of breed, however—in the case of the Palomino, Apaloosa and Pinto, color is the deciding factor.
Reins.	The straps connecting the bridle with the rider's hands.
Romal.	In western tack, a quirt attached to the reins.
Saddle horn.	The projection on the pommel of a western saddle, originally used to hold the lariat.

Seat.	The position of a horseman in the saddle. The term refers to the entire body, not just to the part in contact with the saddle.
Sire.	The male parent of a horse.
Slow-gait.	A man-made gait, slow and gliding, also called the amble and the running walk.
Snaffle.	A bit which is jointed in the middle.
Stallion.	An uncastrated male horse.
Star-gazer.	A horse that holds his head too high, with his nose in the air.
Stirrup.	The support for the rider's foot.
Stirrup leathers.	The straps fastening the stirrups to the saddle.
Stock.	A stock horse and a stock saddle are so called because they were originally used for working with cattle, or stock.
Tack.	The assemblage of equipment used in riding: saddle, bridle, pad, martingale, girth, stirrups, etc.
Throat latch.	The part of the bridle passing under the horse's throat.
Trot.	A moderate (about 6 miles per hour) gait in which the legs move in diagonal pairs.
Walk.	A slow gait (about 3 miles per hour), in which the feet are only slightly removed from the ground.
Walk-trot.	Refers to a horse that walks, trots and canters only, and is not schooled in man-made gaits.
Withers.	The ridge between the shoulder bones of a horse.

Before You Begin

You are a new member of the fast-growing body of horse enthusiasts. Something has sparked your interest in horses: a horse show, television, a parade, or seeing your friends ride. You may actually have been on a horse already, but without proper guidance and supervision.

Are you aware that there are three riding styles, or seats, in popular use? If you are, perhaps you already have a preference for one of the three—either the hunt seat or the saddle seat, both employing forms of the English saddle, or the stock seat, which requires the western saddle.

Each of the three styles is best suited to a certain type of horse. Each has a special set of disciplines and demands the use of a distinct assortment of tack (saddle, bridle, pad, etc.). For each seat there is an appropriate style of clothing.

The purpose of this book is to acquaint you with the fundamentals of learning to ride each of the three seats; with the various breeds of horses; and with the proper tack and outfit for each style. If you are an absolute beginner you will naturally learn to ride in one style first—but it is well for you to know something about the others. If you have already begun riding in one style, you may be interested in mastering one or both of the others—especially if you own, or have access to, a versatile horse. Versatility is now a big thing in the riding world, and if the horse which you customarily ride will go equally well in English or western tack, you will naturally wish to use his talents to the utmost.

The first thing you must do is to familiarize yourself with the names for the various parts of the horse's body and the pieces of equipment which enable you to control him. You must also know the terminology of equitation: what aids are, for example, and that in mounting the horse one does so from the "near" (left) side of the animal. It is also well to have some knowledge of the defects in a horse's structure and the names for them.

To help you, a glossary is provided at the beginning of this book. A chart of the horse's body and also one showing faults are provided, as well as diagrams labelling the various pieces of tack. Study these diagrams and the glossary and refer to them as you proceed into the book.

As everyone knows, a knowledge of horses was widespread in the centuries before the invention of the railroad and the automobile. In earlier days, young people were acquainted with the terminology of horsemanship, knowing the names of the parts of the horse's body and of the equipment needed to ride or drive him, in much the same way as nowadays they know the parts of an automobile.

Everyone knows the difference between a good motorist and a poor one. But now that riding horses has become chiefly a form of recreation (and an increasingly popular one) there are far too many beginners who think that riding is just a matter of climbing on a horse and away. Riding is an involved and complicated discipline. There are right ways and wrong ways to go about it.

Therefore, the following recommendations, applying to all styles of riding, should be heeded:

1. Learn to ride in an enclosure.

2. Have a good instructor.

3. When not in an enclosure, be sure that you are accompanied by experienced riders.

4. Bear in mind that the horse is a living intelligent creature, not a machine.

5. Strive to maintain a light, but sure contact with the horse at all times. Leave the hard riding for the movies.

6. When your feet are in the stirrups, always keep your heels down.

7. Be constantly aware that equitation, the art of riding, like all arts, requires discipline.

8. Accept the fact that all styles of riding, including western, have traditions, and a list of do's and don't's. Respect these.

9. Practice. Long practice is the path to true horsemanship, to achieving the harmonious union of horse and rider.

1. The Three Seats

THE HUNT SEAT

The singular thrill of being able to put a horse over a substantial fence and gallop down to the next one is reason enough for most people to be enthusiastic about learning to ride the traditional hunt seat. Riding hunters and jumpers

The Hunt Seat

creates courageous riders whose form and abilities often gain them international fame. Thousands more are content to enjoy the excitement of speed and flight with their horses without seeking renown.

But before the inviting walls and gates and coops lure you, half-prepared, into the world of the advanced rider, you must have a sound understanding of basic equitation and be able to control your horse in the accepted manner. To achieve the most enjoyment from your horse, you must know why he does or does not perform correctly. You must learn how important good hands are to his performance; how your position in the saddle can help or hinder him over fences; how your being able to rate him will help improve his style as well as your own.

The hunt seat is perhaps the most exacting of the three seats and there are few exceptions to the time-honored rules for the rider of hunters. Tack and apparel have traditional standards which have changed little over the years and require a certain adherence to detail. So, if you are bent on this style of riding, you should familiarize yourself with its demands. Conformity has few opponents in the hunt field!

Once you have decided that this is the way you wish to ride and are prepared to follow the precedents set by custom, your enjoyment will be greater than that of one who takes up a slapdash style. Some of the formality of the hunt seat may seem formidable at first but once you understand the reasons for many of the customs, they will seem both logical and practical.

At the start, of course, you will learn to ride on the flat—that is, without hurdles. A basically secure seat must be acquired àt the walk, trot, and canter before you will be ready to begin jumping. You must endeavor to develop sensitive hands. Without them you cannot be a really capable rider. Your balance and responsiveness will be attained on the flat before you are ready to advance to the jumping stage. All the fundamental requirements of seat and hands should be firmly established before popping over any fences.

But riding hunt seat certainly is not always all formality. There are few thrills to equal a cross-country jaunt with a group of enthusiastic riders, jumping everything in sight and dashing along at an exhilarating gallop. The fields open up before you; the rush of the wind is in your ears, you hear the rhythmic beat of hooves in the grass and feel a sense of oneness with your horse as the miles roll beneath his feet. It crosses your mind, as field and fence flash by, that anyone who has not experienced this thrill has missed something of importance.

Your impressions of the sights and sounds and scents of the open country from a horse's back can be duplicated in no other way.

Only through a sound program of basic equitation can a person gain the skill which enables him to enjoy the complete range of hunt seat activities, from hacking cross-country to Olympic jumping.

THE STOCK SEAT

Although each seat has its legions of supporters and no one seat really dominates the others, there has been a tremendous upsurge of interest in western riding in recent years. Whether television or movies or the lure of stylish riding

The Stock Seat

clothes is responsible for this is not important—all have contributed. Another factor is the increasing popularity of the purebred horses, such as the Quarter Horse, the Morgan and the Arabian, best suited to the stock seat.

It is a fact that more and more people identify with cowboys! Inspired by the television series and even commercials, they fancy themselves tall in the saddle, galloping off into the sunset. They decide, with free time becoming more and more available, that they must ride a horse. They probably have no idea how many hours must be spent in the saddle acquiring a good seat or realize how much ability is needed to get a good performance from their horse.

Put aside those day dreams of galloping into the sunset until the basics have been learned and you and your horse have reached a certain degree of equanimity. What looks worse than a novice rider with more bravado than brains, sticking his horse with evil-looking spurs and tearing about with flapping elbows and legs all askew? He and his horse may be in some form of contact with each other but true harmony with the animal is completely lacking. He may be called a rider by some, but he is not a horseman in any sense.

Too many newcomers to western riding think that they have learned to ride stock seat if they can sit a horse in a stock saddle at all gaits. The characteristics of the saddle itself have given them a sense of security from the start (something to hang on to when the going gets tough!) And soon, with increased confidence in themselves and their ability, they are ready to conquer the world. But only a small percentage of these self-taught riders have truly mastered the stock seat. Until there exists a rapport between horse and rider where they function as an entity, true mastery of the seat has yet to be accomplished.

When you see the stock seat performed by an experienced and sensitive rider on a well-schooled, responsive horse, you realize just how impressive this riding style can be. The difference between this seat well-performed and the week-end "drug-store cowboy" style is as night and day! The flapping arms, the everywhere-at-a-mad-gallop school of thought and the gaudy clothes have no place with the serious western rider. He is most interested in teaching his horse to perform smoothly at each gait, with its neck and head relaxed and its mouth quiet. He realizes this is achieved only by hours of careful training, both for himself and his horse, plus perseverence and an honest desire to succeed. Anyone who truly wishes to be a top western rider must abandon the idea that riding TV style is the method.

Although there may be many excellent riders (even horsemen) in some of the television series, the demand of the scripts for continuous action has a tendency to underplay the riders' ability as horsemen in the equitation sense. Many of the "heroes" have excellent seats, although their hands sometimes have a tendency toward heaviness, due most likely to the demands for exaggerated turns and the inevitable fast starts and sliding stops required by the screenplay.

So, while you may have been inspired by the apparent brilliance of film and television stars as horsemen, pattern your riding on less flamboyant performances.

You must decide that riding stock seat, while definitely good sport, should be considered as exacting a style as hunt or saddle seat. The days are over when, both in the show ring and on the bridle path, riding western was looked down upon the full length of one's nose! Performed properly, it today ranks in importance with other styles in the field of equitation.

THE SADDLE SEAT

Though comparatively new in its present form and lacking, perhaps, some of the romantic tradition of the hunt seat and the historical sentiment of the "seat of the cowboys," the saddle seat is nonetheless making substantial headway in the sport of riding. Having evolved from the seat used on the plantation horses of old Kentucky and Tennessee, it was developed along with the American Saddlebred Horse himself.

Today the saddle seat calls for a certain poise and gracefulness on the part of the rider, as well as extremely sensitive hands and a firm but light seat. Developed and perfected in recent years, it is primarily designed to enhance the appearance and performance of the horse in the show ring. However, its popularity is increasing, and the saddle seat now finds great favor with the pleasure rider. Not only the Saddlebred Horse, but breeds such as the Morgan and the Arabian, have adopted the saddle seat as their accepted style in English tack.

Although Morgans and Arabians can be ridden hunt seat, and perform well in this field, they are generally considered "three-gaited" horses when used on the flat. More and more, they are being ridden saddle seat by show exhibitors and pleasure riders alike. There have been outstanding jumpers and hunters among the two breeds, but nowadays, in general, it is thought more appropriate to ride both Morgans and Arabians saddle seat, with the required tack, than

The Saddle Seat

with the shorter stirrup used in the hunt seat. They just seem to give a better appearance with the rider mounted in this fashion.

Actually, both Arabians and Morgans are extremely versatile breeds and are ridden stock seat, too, looking and performing extremely well in this style. But, to repeat, when these breeds are ridden with English tack, the saddle seat is considered correct. There are a few people who take exception to this as far as Arabians are concerned. With the Morgan horse, however, the saddle seat is almost unanimously accepted. The few die-hards who still ride Morgans hunt seat usually do so because of deep-rooted habit.

The saddle seat is not unlike the stock seat in positioning the rider in the saddle. A longer stirrup is used and the rider's weight is thrown farther back than in the hunt seat. This position was developed because it most enhances the high-headed, big-fronted conformation of the Saddlebred Horse. Morgans, especially, and Arabians, too, have the higher neck and head carriage which is quite unlike the hunter type of horse. A horse which has a lofty bearing looks better with his rider positioned in the saddle seat. The two simply go together.

For pleasure riding, the saddle seat is every bit as satisfactory as the other styles. However, if you are anticipating any great amount of jumping on the trail, other than simple trail obstacles, then perhaps a modified saddle seat with an appropriate saddle would be preferred by some riders. We have ridden quite comfortably cross-country all day in a cut-back show saddle and have found nothing to criticize in the saddle or the seat for this purpose.

Your choice of the saddle seat would probably be most influenced by the locality in which you live and the type of horses most popular in that particular area. If most horse owners rode hunters you would probably be inclined to own a hunter yourself. But if there were more Saddlebreds and Saddlebred types as well as Morgans and Arabians in your area, you would do well to consider learning to ride saddle seat and acquiring a horse of appropriate type. The various popular breeds will be discussed later.

2. Light Horse Breeds

Although you probably will be unlikely to choose an expensive purebred horse with which to learn to ride, sooner or later when you have mastered the art, you will be itching for a really good horse. It is inevitable. In any case, you should acquaint yourself with some of the light horse breeds and their characteristics to help you decide which appeals to you most.

THE THOROUGHBRED

Bred for the race track for over two centuries, the Thoroughbred is nonetheless a magnificent hunter, bridle-path hack, show horse or polo mount. He has a long stride and beautifully smooth gaits. It is said that he has more "heart" than other breeds and his size and substance lends itself to the taller, heavier rider.

Many people choose to ride a Thoroughbred over all others. A great number of breeders use Thoroughbred stallions strictly as "hunter sires," and Thoroughbreds are used extensively for the hunt field and show ring as well as for the track.

Their jumping ability is a well-known in-born characteristic—Thoroughbreds have dominated hunter and jumper events at horse shows all over the world for years. Their excellence as hunters and jumpers is probably unsurpassed.

The blood of the Thoroughbred when crossed on other breeds and grade stock has resulted in the general improvement of gait and conformation in the offspring. One of the most beautiful of horses, the Thoroughbred is held in very high esteem all over the world.

THE ARABIAN

The oldest of the horse breeds, the Arabian is an ancestor of all other established light horse breeds. Down through the ages his type and characteristics have remained unchanged, though his blood flows in the veins of many diversified strains.

The Arabian is one of the most versatile of horses. Though comparatively

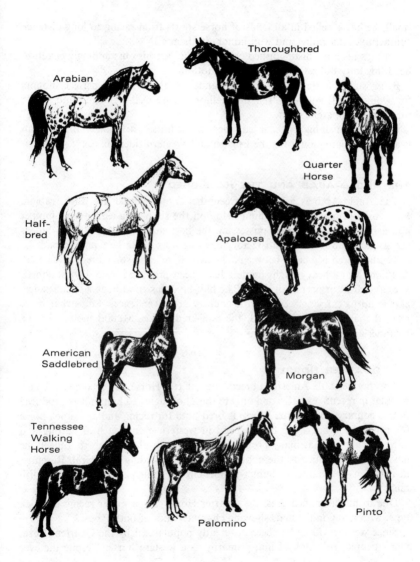

Arabian

Thoroughbred

Quarter Horse

Half-bred

Apaloosa

American Saddlebred

Morgan

Tennessee Walking Horse

Palomino

Pinto

small, he has excelled in all fields of horse sports from racing to long-distance competitive trail riding and won honors in them all.

Perhaps his most distinguished characteristics are his outstandingly beautiful head, his lofty tail set and his graceful motion.

Being small in stature—14.1–15.1 hands—Arabians make perfect mounts for women and children, even the stallions being well-mannered and gentle for all their apparent spirit.

One of the most highly-regarded breeds in the horse world today, the Arabian is an appropriate mount for the English and Western rider alike.

THE ANGLO-ARAB AND THE HALF-BRED

The Anglo-Arab is a cross between the Thoroughbred and the Arabian. He is bred primarily for the hunt field and the show ring as a hunter-jumper and a hunter hack. Usually possessing the best characteristics of both breeds the Anglo-Arab is a very satisfactory pleasure horse both here and abroad.

The half-bred is a cross between a Thoroughbred and some breed other than Arabian. Many heavyweight hunters have been produced from Thoroughbred sires and draft or part-draft dams. The half-bred has good bone and substance, and is up to carrying weight cross-country and over fences. Somewhat more relaxed than the Thoroughbred, the half-bred makes a good mount for the beginner and intermediate rider.

THE QUARTER HORSE

Another versatile American breed, the Quarter Horse has become extremely popular in recent years. Second only to the Thoroughbred in numbers produced in this country, the Quarter Horse is bred both for racing and as a stock horse for ranch and rodeo. He has excelled in western events such as cutting and barrel racing and has many promoters as a western pleasure horse. Indeed, he has contributed much to the popularity of western riding in general. Recently, he has even moved into the hunter-jumper circles, going perfectly well in English tack.

Due to his diversified uses, the Quarter Horse can be either racing or stock type, with many individuals showing characteristics of both types.

Since western riding has been so greatly popularized by the Quarter Horse, many people still think of him primarily as a western horse. Despite the ever

22

increasing demand for racing-type Quarter Horses, the breed finds his greatest use in the field of western pleasure riding.

THE MORGAN HORSE

America's first native horse breed, dating back to the 1700's, the Morgan began with just one extraordinary little stallion known as Justin Morgan. From this small (14 hands) bay stud sprang this distinctive and beautiful stock.

Today ranging in size from 14.1–15.1 hands, the Morgan is often called the "big-little" horse. His fame as an amazingly versatile breed is well known in the horse world. Within his ranks have been produced brilliant show horses with beautiful action, as well as perfect all-around pleasure horses for riders of all ages.

A naturally stylish animal with a characteristic sprightly way of going and a personality unexcelled, the Morgan is the horse for everyone!

In the show ring he exhibits the lofty, stylish action of the park horse both in Fine Harness events and under saddle. He has likewise won favor with ranch owners as a stock horse. He looks equally well in either English or Western tack and as a pleasure-driving horse he is without equal.

Because of his smooth symmetry and regal carriage, the Morgan, once seen, is seldom forgotten. He makes the ideal family horse, being friendly and agreeable in disposition and of a size practical for all.

THE AMERICAN SADDLEBRED

Developed in old Kentucky, the Saddlebred was intended primarily to be a smooth-gaited plantation horse, outstanding because of his style, lofty bearing and comfortable gaits.

Founded on lines of Thoroughbred, Morgan and Canadian pacer origin, the Saddlebred is today not only the peacock of the show ring but an excellent pleasure horse as well. He has the size and smoothness of gait of the Thoroughbred, the showy attitude inherited from his Morgan forebears and the high, stylish action and symmetry which is his own hallmark. Quality and refinement are in his every line, the Saddlebred having been bred for beauty as well as performance from his early beginnings.

The Saddlebred is divided into two classifications: the Three-gaited or, as he is known among his supporters, the "Walk-Trot"; and the Five-Gaited, known simply as the "Gaited horse." His gaits are the natural walk, trot, and canter, and the artificial, man-made ones: the slow-gait and the rack.

Because of his comfortable way of going, the Saddlebred has many enthusiasts among the pleasure horse fraternity, as well as being the undisputed star of the show ring.

THE TENNESSEE WALKING HORSE

Another breed developed in America, the Tennessee Walking Horse has gained popularity in recent years both as a show horse and as a pleasure horse.

Famous for the running walk which gave him his name, this horse, too, was founded on Morgan, Thoroughbred and Canadian pacer lines. Along with a remarkably placid disposition, the Walking Horse has gaits which appeal to the less athletic horseman. In size, he is a comparatively large horse, up to any weight, and makes the ideal pleasure horse for the older rider of limited ability.

The Walking Horse is also a well-known show ring preformer where his speedy running walk and rocking-horse canter are unique among all entries.

In size the Walking Horse stands from 15.2–16.2 hands. He has great depth of shoulder, a shapely neck and good bone. When trained for pleasure, he makes a satisfactory horse for the beginner who desires to ride on the flat with the least amount of effort! Since the Walking Horse does not trot, there is no need to learn to post which may or may not be a disadvantage.

THE APALOOSA, THE PALOMINO, THE PINTO

These are the so-called color "breeds." Horses with varied bloodlines can be found with Palomino or Pinto coats or the exotic spotted patterns of the Apaloosa. The registries of the color breeds are all striving continually to improve type, conformation and performance of their respective breeds.

The Apaloosa, originally developed by the Nez Perce Indians of the Pacific Northwest is considered to be basically a stock horse type. Much Quarter Horse blood has been introduced into the breed in recent years in an effort to improve conformation and type. The distinctive color patterns of the Apaloosa contribute much to his popularity.

The Palomino can be a horse of any good breed type with his eligibility for registry dependent upon his color. Palominos of the best color are the shade of a newly minted gold coin; or three shades lighter or darker. Well-known as parade horses, the many beautiful Palominos seen today are mainly derived from Arabian, Quarter Horse, Saddlebred and Morgan blood.

One of the most recent color breeds to establish its own registry is the Pinto. By no means new, however, the Pinto has been treading American soil since the time of the Conquistadors. Usually thought of as the typical Indian pony, Pintos, with their flashy patterns of color have always been found in films and on television. Now they are becoming more and more in demand for all-round pleasure horses as well as for shows and circuses.

They are equally adaptable to English or Western tack. Some have made outstanding hunters; others, flashy saddle-type show horses. Another of the versatile breeds, the Pinto lends himself well to any sort of training. And, as his promoters exclaim, "He will never be lost in a crowd!"

3. Tack, Clothing and Horses

HUNT SEAT TACK AND OUTFIT

When you have mulled it all over in your mind, when you have studied the horse breeds and their qualifications, and when you have finally decided to which seat you will devote your riding time, your next undertaking will be to avail yourself of the proper tack.

At first thought, this may seem like a simple pleasure. But wait till you see the assortment of tack available! The variety is seemingly endless today. Both in perusing the saddle catalogs or roaming through the many tack shops which have sprung up in almost every locality, the novice is faced with so many items that take his eye, that usually confusion almost to the point of complete exasperation results and makes any choices extremely difficult.

How do you find the right saddle, the correct bridle, the accessories from the multitudes displayed?

First, you have a clear idea of the type of equipment used by the seat you have chosen. Then you must fit yourself and your horse with the proper style. Keep in mind your horse's conformation when picking a saddle—it must fit him correctly as well as fit you. Select a bridle with the proper bit or bits in the right mouth size (width of mouthpiece) for your horse. If possible, it would be best if you took along someone who is experienced to advise you. Sometimes the mind boggles at the sight of so much tack all in one place!

Today almost everyone interested in hunters and jumpers rides a forward seat saddle. There are several variations on the market today. English, German, Italian, Argentine and domestic. As a beginner, however, the more elaborate Olympic jumping saddle is more saddle than you will need at this time.

Occasionally, you may have an opportunity to pick up a used forward seat saddle that is completely broken in, that will be an advantageous buy, provided it has been well-cared for and is in sound condition. The billets should be in the very best condition, as should the stirrup leathers and girth, if included. Inspect it carefully if you anticipate purchasing it. If it is in good condition, it will be better than a new one, which would have to be broken in with care over a period of time. If possible, sit in any saddle before you buy it. It is important that it fits you and be completely comfortable for you.

Illustrated are several saddles correctly used on the hunter type horse. The use of an all-purpose saddle is quite permissible on the hunter, too. Inexpensive Argentine models are available in all styles for those with limited funds.

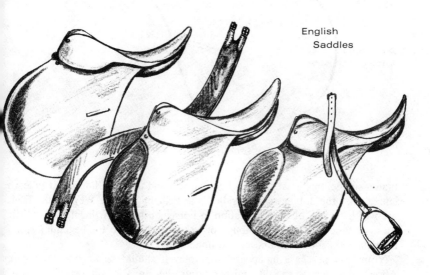

English Saddles

There are various quite inexpensive English-style saddles, such as semi-military. But learning to ride hunt seat correctly is better accomplished in the forward seat saddle or modified forward seat saddle. The concealed knee rolls afford a secure seat, while the higher cantle positions the rider more correctly for this riding style. The most important factor, however, is a proper fit to the rider. Bear this in mind when acquiring your saddle.

The type of bridle you will need depends on the horse you select. Some horses need more restraint than others, thus the need for the various bits and bit combinations illustrated here. If you have a horse which needs nothing more

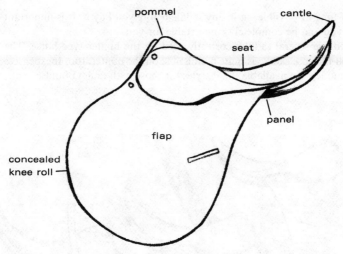

Forward Seat Saddle

than a snaffle, this is satisfactory but bear in mind that it is important to learn later to use the double reined bridles: the Pelham and the Weymouth. Their use will be a part of your education in horsemanship. Martingales have their uses on some horses and, although of less importance to the beginning rider, their function should be understood nonetheless.

Your first purchase in apparel for yourself should be a good hunt cap. Affording protection should a mishap occur, they are also comfortable to wear. (And incidentally, almost everyone looks well in one!) The hard variety is the only one to consider. The soft velvet caps are strictly for style and offer no protection whatever. A hard hunt derby, of course, is correct, too, but most riders, especially juniors, usually prefer the hunt cap to the derby.

High boots are your next consideration. They come in a number of price ranges and should fit properly not only the foot, but the calf of the leg as well. Since nothing looks worse than ill-fitting boots, choose them carefully. If you are ordering by mail, always send accurate leg measurements. High boots are recommended for the beginner as they offer protection as well as providing better contact with the saddle and thus a more secure seat.

Although leather boots are best, wet weather riding boots are available in black rubber or the popular Newmarket style. They are practical and give a good appearance for everyday riding as well.

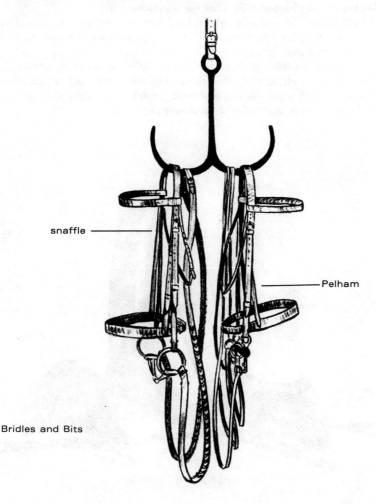

snaffle

Pelham

Bridles and Bits

To begin with, you may wish to wear a turtleneck jersey or sweater with your breeches and boots instead of a shirt, tie and jacket. Hunt style jodhpurs and "jod" boots, too, are both comfortable and correct for general riding. Gloves are always proper but their use is optional here.

Riding coats of tweed or solid colors, worn usually with a white shirt, a stock tie or choker are correct for hacking or showing. Breeches in canary yellow or buff and the high boots complete the outfit.

It is important that your riding clothes be well-fitting and comfortable. They need not be expensive while you are learning, but they should be neat and not flashy. Later on when you might consider hunting or showing your horse, you may wish to avail yourself of a made-to-measure outfit.

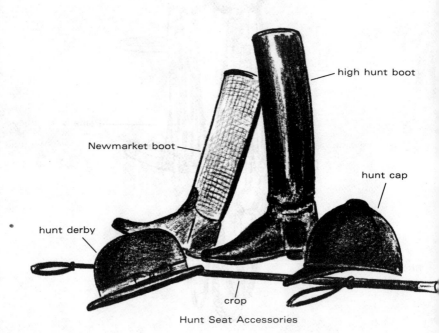

Hunt Seat Accessories

Hunt Seat Apparel

CHOOSING A HORSE FOR THE HUNT SEAT

In choosing a horse for a beginner, disposition should be the first consideration, with good training right on its heels in importance. The hunter type horse you select can be half or part Thoroughbred or a useful grade horse of good general conformation. Again, a bit of age is advantageous if the horse is steady and reliable. The illustrations show some horses suitable for hunt seat equitation. Avoid the star-gazer, the extremely heavy chunk or the Thoroughbred off the race track. They all have their problems and do not make suitable mounts for beginners.

Hunter-type Horses

Of course, a good mouth is important: a horse with a mouth as hard and unresponsive as an anvil is of no value. A beginner has neither the wit nor the strength to cope with this sort. Neither do you want a horse with a fussy, overly-sensitive mouth, as he is easily upset by a beginner's unsteady hands and will become nervous and flighty. His behavior tends to shake the confidence of the new rider while it is still in the formative stage.

The beginner's horse should have agreeable gaits. The trot, particularly, should have a rhythmic cadence to facilitate the rider's learning to post. And the canter must be easily controllable by unsure hands. A headstrong, rank animal needs the experience of the professional, so even if he really fills your eye with his appearance and spirit, forget him. He is not for you as a beginner.

However, you possibly will want, even at the outset, a horse with some jumping ability for your future enjoyment. So, if possible, have the horse you are considering put over a few fences by an experienced rider so you may see how he handles himself. Then, when you have advanced to the jumping stage, you know you will have a horse which will be capable of at least starting with you in this phase of horsemanship.

STOCK SEAT TACK AND OUTFIT

If you have elected to ride stock seat, you will look at western tack carefully. Do not buy the first fancy saddle you see just because its decoration has caught your eye. Many fall into this trap only to regret it later.

If you are buying by catalog from a reputable maker of western equipment, you may want to have your saddle made to your measure. There are usually blanks for this included in the catalog. If not, sending a list of your measurements—height, weight, etc.—will be helpful in assuring you of a saddle that will fit you properly and in which you will be comfortable. Remember, the best looking saddle in the world can be a torture chamber if it does not fit you correctly. It is very important that you choose your saddle wisely. With good care, it can last you a long, long time.

A saddle does not necessarily have to be very expensive to be right for you. However, the range in price is enormous today, so choose carefully, keeping in the back of your mind that your dollar is best spent on top quality saddlery.

Ideally, you should try to buy your stock saddle in person where you can try it on one of the display horses in the shop. Then you will have the feel of it and how it will position you on your horse. Be sure the stirrups are free swinging

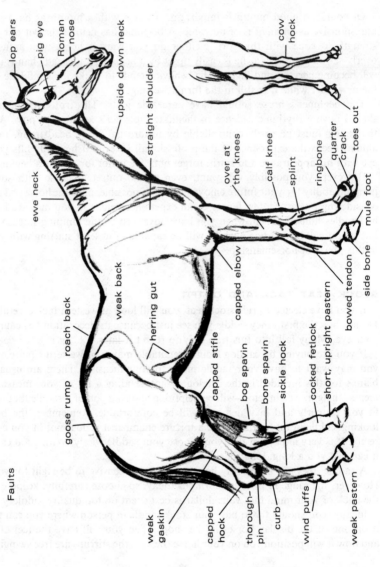

Faults

lop ears
pig eye
Roman nose
upside down neck
straight shoulder
cow hock
ewe neck
over at the knees
calf knee
splint
ringbone
quarter crack
toes out
mule foot
side bone
bowed tendon
weak back
capped elbow
herring gut
short, upright pastern
cocked fetlock
roach back
goose rump
capped stifle
bog spavin
bone spavin
sickle hock
weak gaskin
capped hock
thorough-pin
curb
wind puffs
weak pastern

34

Stock Seat Saddles

so that your legs are comfortable. There is probably nothing worse than to find, when riding your new saddle for the first time, that the way the fenders are hung puts a terrible strain on your knees, leading to extreme discomfort. The importance of a correctly fitting stock saddle, which means so much to your enjoyment of western riding, cannot be overemphasized.

If you must order your saddle by mail, of course the made-to-measure type is best. But most reputable catalog companies will send you a saddle out of stock which will fit you, if you include your measurements with your order.

Now that the importance of proper fit has been stressed, style and appearance are next. Here is where the great range in price occurs. So many really beautiful stock saddles are being made today by craftsmen of several firms, that making a choice is quite difficult sometimes. It is a matter of preference whether you wish to indulge yourself in flower-carving and buck-stitching or lean toward the conservative, workmanlike, rough-out or stitched latigo.

We have illustrated several types, all perfectly suitable for western pleasure riding. Provided they fit you right and are comfortable to both you and your horse, any one of them would be a good choice.

The styles of western saddles and equipment seem to change greatly in affluent society. Certain fads come and go constantly in western fashion. This

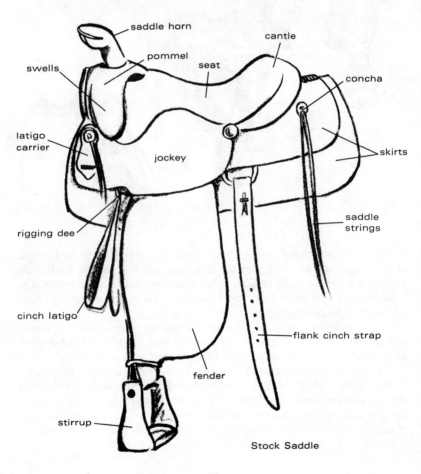

Stock Saddle

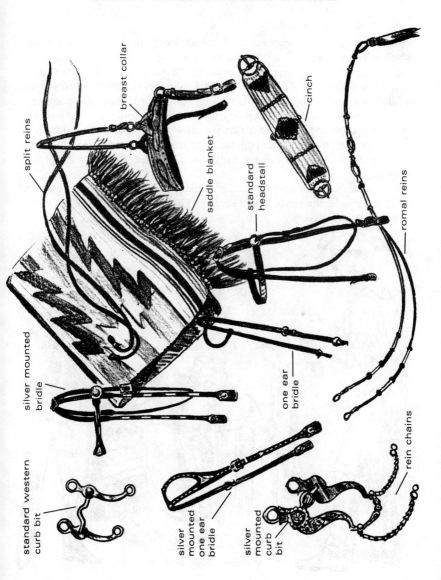

breast collar

split reins

cinch

saddle blanket

standard headstall

romal reins

silver mounted bridle

one ear bridle

rein chains

standard western curb bit

silver mounted one ear bridle

silver mounted curb bit

makes the tack shops happy but it is difficult for the novice who must decide which is fad and which is a sound investment.

One does not see, for example, as many of the rough-out work saddles today as ten years ago. The buck-stitching and flower carving are "in." Headstalls (bridles) are of fine leather and often silver trimmed with narrow cheekpieces; the aim is to put as little as necessary on the horse's head. One-ear headstalls have been popular with western riders everywhere. The California influence, too, has brought to nationwide popularity the romal rein and the silver-mounted bit. The various styles in demand today are illustrated. Each is correct. It is a matter of preference.

Accessories, such as colorful saddle blankets, breast collars, fancy cinches, again come under the heading of preference. You may outfit yourself as lavishly

Western Tack and Apparel

as you wish. But keeping an eye on the items which are currently "in" is advisable! Beware of black-dyed leather and nickel spots, wide-cheeked bridles and high-cantled saddles. They are definitely "out"! But who knows when they may be "in."

Western fashions being so very popular with even non-riders today, it is equally difficult to outfit yourself and not go overboard on styles, too. The choices in clothes are almost unbelievable. Just keeping up with them is a problem!

For everyday western pleasure riding, jeans still head the list in popularity. Today they come in a variety of colors for both men and women—children, too—and are cut with narrow legs for riding comfort. Floppy, wide-legged pants are definitely not advisable for riding, as they tend to ride up and bunch around the knees, causing painful chafes. If you like the currently fashionable bell-bottom pants, make sure they fit snugly around the calves so they stay where they belong.

Western boots are a must, and again they can be as fancy or as plain as you wish, but they should be comfortable and well-made.

The styles in western shirts and hats are endless. Just use your good taste in choosing them! Chaps seem to be very popular, too, especially with the "show crowd." Shotgun styles are being worn by most riders.

A word of caution on all this western fashion: don't be too dazzled by it all at this stage. You can easily go all out on your "image" as a western rider when learning to ride correctly should take precedence over all else.

As a novice in the world of the horse, you will find that the things you must learn seem to come at you from all directions, with questions, questions, questions, arising at every turn. Keep cool. Your understanding will increase with your experience if you use plain common sense in dealing with any problems which may arise.

CHOOSING A STOCK HORSE

In choosing your first horse, you will want all your wits about you. For the sound choice of the first horse can put you literally on the highway to equine adventure with enjoyment increasing daily. The selection of an unsuitable animal leads to exasperation, frustration and eventual complete disillusionment with the whole project.

So select him wisely.

Stock Horses

The first rule to remember: don't purchase a young horse unfinished in his training unless you are going to have qualified or professional help with you at *all* times. Even then, the case of two greenhorns, equine and human, trying to teach each other, is truly one of the halt leading the blind. It is seldom a satisfactory arrangement and *never* one to undertake without professional help.

Young horses learn quickly—both right and wrong—and habits once acquired are difficult if not impossible, to break, leading to a spoiled horse and a disappointed rider.

While it is natural that you would like to have a horse of whose appearance you can be proud, remember his disposition and training count for much more at this stage. You should try to find an animal with some age and enough training to be responsive without being "hot." Many horses at 9 or 10 years of age are excellent mounts for the beginner.

Although you do not want a "plug" who is too lazy to be of much use, neither do you want a "fireball" who is just too much horse for you.

When searching for your first horse it is advisable to take along a qualified horseman or woman who will help you by pointing out faults and undesirable characteristics which you might be apt to overlook. A basic knowledge of a few of the more common complaints to which a horse is subject is a necessity as well. A chart showing some of these troubles appears on page 34. It would be beneficial if you studied it to familiarize yourself with the problems, should you encounter them in any of your prospects.

For western pleasure riding you will want a horse—we would suggest a good gelding—with smooth gaits. He should not have a bone-jarring jog, nor a lope which is too fast and too strong. He should neck-rein well and have a reasonably responsive mouth. In size, he should be not much over 15 hands (unless you are very tall and heavy and *need* a larger horse). All these points should come before looks. The horse should be free of any unsoundness in wind or limb.

strip

star and snip

blaze

bald face

Head Markings

Blemishes, such as wire cuts or wind puffs (small, rubbery bumps on the fetlock joint), if they do not affect his soundness, are of little consequence here. If possible, have him ridden, preferably by your horseman friend, so you may see how he performs.

While a western pleasure horse does not need to excel at sliding stops or cutting fancy maneuvers, he should be agile and alert to give the best ride. However, leave the real reining horse to the experienced rider, or you may find him too quick for you. A horse that has had a great deal of advanced training will be more horse than, as a beginner, you will require. Some stock horses are as quick as deer when given certain cues. They can easily leave a beginner (and some advanced riders, too!) sitting on air if reined inadvertently.

SADDLE SEAT TACK AND OUTFIT

There is something about sitting on the back of a high-headed Saddlebred or Morgan that is reminiscent of a knight upon his grand, proud war horse, about to ride off into battle. There is something about the lofty carriage and showy gait to make the rider feel 10 feet tall! Perhaps it is this characteristic of the saddle type horse that has drawn people to him and to the style of riding required by him. If you aspire to riding only on the flat, yet want something of the thrill of jumping, the saddle seat and the type of horse that it goes with are exactly suited to you.

Although admittedly developed for the show ring, the saddle seat is definitely becoming equally at home in the park or on the trail: many riders prefer it to the others, usually because of the type of horse they have chosen.

The tack used in conjunction with the saddle seat, although English style, is quite different from the hunt equipment. Because of the completely dissimilar carriage and conformation of the Saddlebred horse, with which it is worn, and the different requirements in performance, a style of equipment has been developed over the past 35 years which not only is original in design, but is as distinctly American as the breed which was responsible for it.

Only a cut-back show saddle is really correct for saddle seat equitation. Modifications of the cut-back are seen, of course, but if one is seriously interested in riding saddle seat correctly, there are really no satisfactory substitutes. Illustrated are three styles, all acceptable: regular skirt, wide skirt and the special equitation saddle which has a deeper seat.

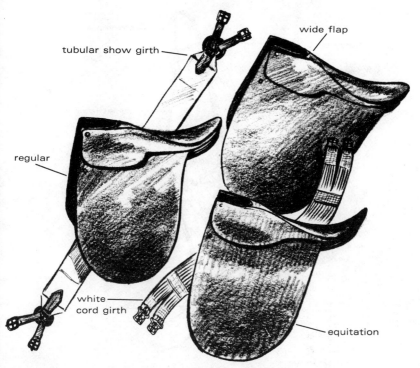

Cut-back Show Saddles

With the cut-back saddle a wide white web girth is used or for everyday use a white cord or mohair girth is recommended. Stirrup irons and leathers are standard English style.

Although the full bridle or show bridle, illustrated here, is correct, the beginner must have its uses carefully explained to him. Ideally, he should have some professional instruction at the outset of learning to ride saddle seat. The basics for this seat will be given in a subsequent chapter.

A good way to begin is to put your horse into a snaffle bridle with two reins fastened into the snaffle bit with the lower rein being run through the rings of a

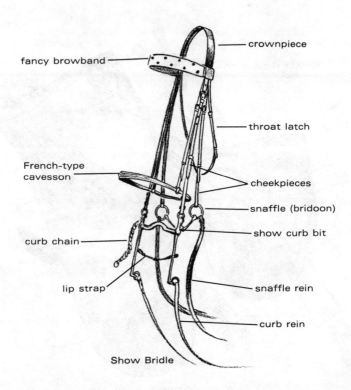

crownpiece

fancy browband

throat latch

French-type
cavesson

cheekpieces

snaffle (bridoon)

show curb bit

curb chain

snaffle rein

lip strap

curb rein

Show Bridle

running martingale. This will give some of the effect of the full bridle—curb and snaffle—without jeopardizing the horse's mouth while the beginner is becoming familiar with the functions of two bits at a time. A detailed explanation of the handling of this arrangement as well as of the full bridle will be given later. The snaffle bridle and martingale, form a necessary part of your equipment.

The use of a colored wide browband is correct on the saddle seat mount so you may use your color preference and dress your horse up in what appeals to you. Matching cavessons are used by some but the stitched leather ones of the so-called French type, seem to be most popular now. Narrow cheek pieces and narrow reins with hook and studs are *always* used on the show bridle. Never use a wide rein with this style. Bits are the show curb—illustrated—and snaffle (bridoon). The length of the shank of the curb bit and the type of bridoon is dependent upon your horse's individual requirements.

While the high riding boots are always correct for hunt seat, never, never are they used when riding saddle seat. Appropriate only are jodhpur boots, usually elastic gore style, and the Kentucky jodhpur.

The Kentucky jods are a relatively recent innovation which have become the only correct riding pants for the saddle seat rider. If you are riding a three-gaited horse (this can include Morgans and Arabians, too) you will feel most correct wearing Kentucky jods. When you are beginning to ride or if you are

Saddle Seat Apparel

riding just around home or on the trail, the jods, boots and a simple riding shirt or sweater are suitable. However, if you are planning to show, the saddle suit is a must today. With coat and jods made of the same material, the saddle suit is a form-fitting garment, flattering to the wearer. The coat is cut longer than the hunt coat and has a flare and inverted side pleats, which give an extremely attractive look when the wearer is on a horse. The flared bell-bottoms of the jods cover the boots to the instep. They should be slightly longer when the wearer is standing on the ground, so that when he is mounted they will come down over the boot heels. Nothing looks worse than Kentucky jods which are too short and are creeping halfway up the rider's leg! Always use the straps which are supplied with the jods to keep the jods where they belong.

If you do not wish to invest in a saddle suit (usually made to measure) you will be perfectly correct in Kentucky jods and a contrasting color coat cut on saddle seat lines. A white coat and black (only) jods are correct or black jods and a red, green, blue or yellow coat can be worn. Avoid the gaudy shades (cerise, peacock blue, orange, etc.) at least until you have become a qualified rider and even then use good judgment. Loud outfits tend to distract rather than enhance.

Headwear is simple: for showing, only a hard saddle derby is correct on the saddle-type horse. (Although in formal night classes at shows it is permissible

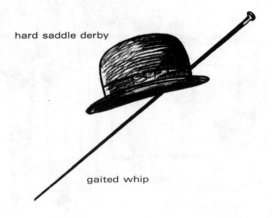

hard saddle derby

gaited whip

46

Saddle
Type
Horses

to wear a top hat on the three-gaited Saddlebred—"walk-trot" horse.) However, for park or pleasure riding, a soft sport hat with a brim can be worn, although it is not necessary to wear a hat at all. Caps are not appropriate at any time.

Very often the rider may wish to carry a crop or whip. A crop is correct on the hunter, but on a saddle-type horse one uses a "gaited whip." This is a longer, more slender whip without a thong or wrist loop. It is very limber and comfortable to hold and quite effective to "pick a horse up a bit" when necessary.

CHOOSING A SADDLE-TYPE HORSE

If you are aiming eventually for saddle seat equitation in the show ring, it is suggested that you learn to ride on a Saddlebred Horse at the start. To get the "feel" of a "heads-up" horse from the beginning, it is best to start with one. A low-headed hunter type or stock horse type will never be suitable to learn to ride saddle seat as their carriage and conformation is totally opposite to that of the Saddlebred. A Morgan, being set up somewhat like a Saddlebred, can be a good beginner's mount and some Arabians, too, may qualify. However, in general a Saddlebred with a good disposition and finished in its training probably is best for the beginner.

For pleasure riding, using the saddle seat, however, any horse that is of general saddle-type (illustrated) makes a good mount for the saddle seat rider. Being admittedly partial to the Morgan, we recommend the breed most heartily. The Arabian is a fine animal, but care must be taken not to acquire too much horse for the beginner's ability. It is a matter of choice, of course, and everyone has his own preferences.

Always keep in mind the basic requirements for a beginner's horse and don't over-mount yourself regardless of the seat you have chosen.

4. Riding Hunt Seat

Snaffle Bridle

It is suggested that for your introduction to riding hunt seat, that your horse be wearing a snaffle bridle. If you have chosen the horse wisely, he will handle perfectly well in a snaffle. If he requires more restraining methods, perhaps he is more horse than you are ready for.

BRIDLING THE HORSE

To bridle your horse, stand on his near (left) side. Put the reins over his head and back on his neck about halfway. Then grasping your bridle at the crownpiece in your left hand, slip it on as shown in the illustration guiding the bit carefully into the horse's mouth with your right hand. If you slip your thumb into the side of his mouth and press upon his lower jaw, he will open up to allow the bit to be put in place. Be careful not to clank the bit against his front teeth. Too much of this is quite apt to make a horse head shy. Go easy. Draw the top of the bridle carefully over his ears. When it is correctly in place, the bit should just touch the corners of his mouth. Next fasten the throat latch; neither too tight nor too loose. Check the illustration.

Hunt Seat: Bridling

Position your saddle as shown. If your horse has extremely high withers, you will have to use a pad to keep the saddle from coming in direct contact with the withers and causing a painful sore.

Adjust the length of the stirrups by the method shown in the illustration. This is an approximation. When you are mounted you may adjust them so that your leg is in a proper and comfortable position for you. Check the girth to be sure it is snug so that the saddle will stay put when you mount. It is wise to pull up the girth before you adjust your stirrups, then go back and tighten it up some more. Many horses, especially the old crafty ones, learn to suck in air and blow up their bellies so that when they exhale the girth will be loose. Always check it again before you mount.

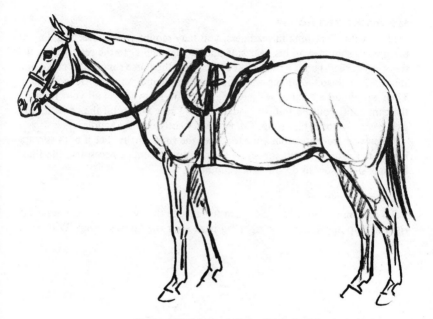

Proper Position of Hunt Seat Saddle

Hunt Seat: Adjusting Stirrups

MOUNTING THE HORSE

Now, with everything in readiness, you may mount your horse. Standing at the horse's shoulder on his near side and facing slightly to the rear, gather the reins in your left hand. Keep light contact with the horse's mouth to make him stand. Then grasp the stirrup with your right hand and put your left foot into it. Then with your left hand (still holding reins) on his withers and your right on the cantle, lift yourself into the saddle, taking care not to hit the horse as you swing your leg over his croup. Come down lightly into the saddle.

When you are seated, put your foot into the right stirrup. See if both stirrups are of the proper length for you. If more adjustment is necessary, the illustrations show how to do this when mounted.

DISMOUNTING

To dismount, and it is a good idea to practice this once or twice, release the right stirrup and bring your right leg back over the horse's croup. With your

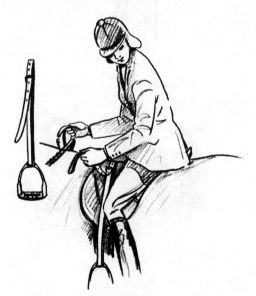

Adjusting Stirrup Length While Mounted

Put left foot in stirrup

weight on your left stirrup and your hands, you are now standing sideways on your horse. Now kick your foot out of the left stirrup and drop slowly to the ground with both feet hitting the ground together. Or instead, you may step down one foot at a time. Practice mounting and dismounting a few times till you can do it with comparative ease. Then remount.

Swing leg over croup

Come down lightly in saddle

Dismounting

ACHIEVING A CORRECT SEAT

To be seated correctly in the forward seat saddle, you must be directly over the horse's center of gravity with your body erect but not stiff. Your head should be up and your shoulders back, but without rigidity, with your upper arms next to your body—never out. Your hands should be over the horse's withers and not too far apart. The knuckles should be at about a 30° angle and the line between the hands and the bit should be straight. This way the horse's head is in a normal and relaxed position, correct for this riding style.

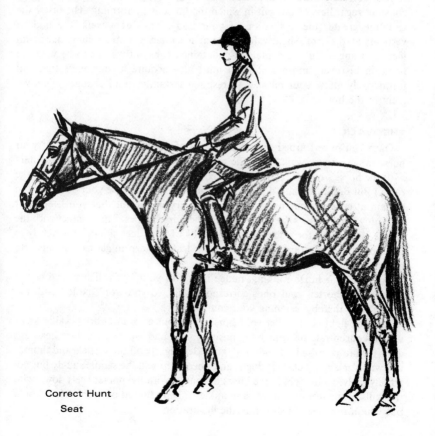

Correct Hunt
Seat

Your legs should grip the saddle with thighs, knees and calves, with the ankles turned in slightly and the heels thrust down in the irons. The illustration shows the basic position in the saddle for the beginner riding hunt seat. Variations of this may come with the special requirements of the advanced rider. Since we are discussing only the beginning rider, the variations will be omitted here.

In any riding style, the rider must be in balance with his horse at all times. If your correct position is maintained in the saddle, you will keep this balance constant regardless of the gait in which the horse is performing. The faster the gait, the greater the inclination of your body. Thus at a walk, the body is vertical; at the trot, slightly forward; at a canter, gallop or jumping, at an increased angle. But leg contact is maintained constantly so as to be with the horse in his every movement. You must also acquire a suppleness that will instinctively allow your muscles to respond instantly to all changes of movement of the horse.

THE WALK

Once you have learned the requirements of position in the saddle, let your horse move off at a walk. With the reins in both hands, ride with light contact with the horse's mouth. (That is, take control by applying light pressure on the reins.) But don't pull and don't stiffen your wrists and tense your body. Try to remain at ease as your horse moves. It is very important that you keep your heels down and your knees snug against the horse's sides. This contact with the saddle is essential for a firm seat. The balls of your feet should rest lightly in the stirrups. Don't turn your feet outward at a sharp angle as this tends to make you lose your knee grip.

To start your horse walking, nudge him with your heels. If his head comes up slightly, shorten your reins correspondingly, so you won't be left with too long a rein, thereby lessening your control.

Keeping light contact, let your horse move out at a fairly brisk walk. As he walks, concentrate on your body position, seat and legs. Remember: head-up; arms next to your body; hands with knuckles slightly off the vertical and thumbs up; wrists relaxed, not stiff; thighs and knees gripping the saddle snugly but not tensely; calves a bit behind the knees in contact with the horse; heels down with the balls of the feet on stirrups and ankles *slightly* turned outward. This should put you in the position shown in the illustration.

The Walk

Turning at a Walk

With your horse walking, coordinate the use of your reins and legs to increase or decrease his speed. If you wish him to move out a bit faster, urge him on by squeezing him with your legs and, if necessary, your heels (lightly, not flaying him with them!) and feel his mouth with the bit. If you "nick" him lightly with one rein then the other, while urging him with your legs, he should increase his speed. Should he start to jig or go on faster than you wish, take back on him with the reins and at the same time sit back (throw your weight back) in the saddle. Practice regulating his walking speed to help yourself understand the effectiveness of the coordination of the aids.

When you wish to turn your horse to the right, you shorten your right rein, applying just enough pressure so that the horse responds. Don't yank. At the same time press your left leg into his side behind the girth. If your horse responds correctly, he will turn freely: his whole body coming around in a straight line not just his head and neck bending with the rein. This is the reason for using your legs as well as your reins when turning. The horse should turn smoothly without "rubbernecking." Practice correct turns to the right and left keeping your horse at a walk.

Backing

To back him up, have him stand. Then "feel" his mouth lightly with the reins. When he feels as though he is responsive to you, give little tugs on the reins with your fingers, at the same time applying light pressure. Say "Back" to him clearly and squeeze him with both legs to keep him backing straight. He should then drop his head slightly in response to the action of the bit and step back quietly. Keep your hands low. Never yank or tug at his mouth to get him to back. If he requires this treatment, he has been spoiled and all your yanking and tugging will only make him throw his head and plant his feet more firmly. A horse which has been soured about backing requires an experienced rider to correct the fault. At this stage, don't *you* attempt to "unspoil" him!

If your horse backs smoothly and straightly, don't keep asking him to do this over and over. It will only sour him and add nothing to your equitation. Just understand how it is done correctly and ask him to back only once or twice a session.

You should keep your horse at a walk until you feel you are successfully meeting the requirements of a firm seat and the use of your basic aids. If your horse is responding passively but consistently, you are still on the right track. Always be aware of his various reactions to the things you ask of him. If he keeps his head down and his mouth quiet and maintains the speed you desire without fretting, you are handling him correctly. If he tosses his head, wears his

Incorrect Reining

ears at an angle (indicating annoyance) and seems unsteady in his way of going, perhaps you have a "death grip" on his mouth or he feels your insecurity in the saddle. Learn to evaluate your own performance as well as his. Once you have learned to feel a mutual coordination with him you know you are being successful.

The best riders never forget that the horse is a living, breathing being, capable of remarkable performances if properly handled. He is not a push-button machine. He feels, he thinks and he responds to given stimuli and the habit of repetition. Understanding fully his limitations as well as his talents is a prerequisite to being an outstanding rider. Naturally, this is not acquired in a few lessons but must be grasped over a period of time: how long depends on your natural aptitude and your affinity for the sport.

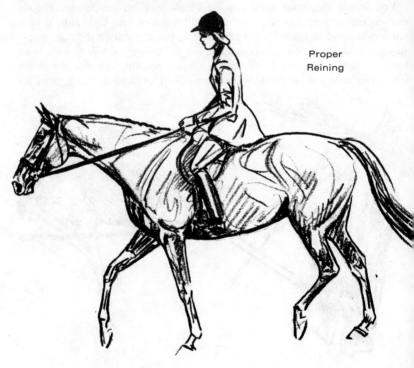

Proper
Reining

A good horse, well-schooled and with an even disposition, can teach his rider far more effectively than one which is either too lazy or too "hot" for the beginner. One thing cannot be stressed enough—the importance of acquiring a true beginner's horse at the outset. Such horses are worth their weight in diamonds regardless of their beauty or lack of it.

Now you are ready to move on to the trot, but only if you can successfully maintain your position in the saddle and control your horse without difficulty. Keeping in mind a mental image of the ideal hunt seat position (as illustrated), endeavor to place yourself in the saddle in this manner and stay in balance with your horse. At first, of course, you will have your difficulties: you will find yourself tipping forward; you will lose contact with your horse's mouth, or you will grab on to it to steady yourself; you will try to keep those heels down and think you'll never be able to and you will clutch the saddle pommel in desperation when you get all out of balance. Cheer up. You *will* master it if you are persistent and determined. Sometimes it will not seem easy but, given time and plenty of practice, you will soon find that the aids become second nature to you and you have begun to work with your horse, not against him. Don't try to hurry. Be thorough. If you feel you have not mastered the first stage, do so before going on.

THE TROT

To start your horse trotting, collect him by shortening your reins alerting him to a change of gait. Use your legs firmly to urge him into his trot. But be subtle. Don't thrash him with them! Urge him to increase his speed by *pressure* not thumping legs.

Your hands should be low and steady on the reins. Do not take a "death grip" on them, as though you were one end of a tug of war, nor let them flop loosely either. Just keep light contact with your horse's mouth to steady *him* (not yourself!).

At first you will keep your horse trotting slowly, sitting to the gait while endeavoring to maintain your seat correctly in the saddle as you hold it at a walk. It is very important that you try to relax and follow the horse's motion. If you keep your horse trotting slowly and collected, he will not jounce you excessively. Concentrate on keeping your seat tight but don't tense up—ride with the punches, as it were! Try to keep your hands from interfering too much with your horse's mouth. If you keep them low you will have less trouble.

Avoid the tendency to "hang on by the reins." If you feel you are becoming insecure in the saddle or losing your balance, bring your horse back to a walk immediately. Regain your seat and begin again. Never yank your horse's mouth to keep yourself in the saddle, if you can avoid it. This is one of the reasons why it is best to use the snaffle bridle until you have acquired a seat: the snaffle is less likely to injure the horse's mouth should you unavoidably yank the reins.

As you slowly trot your horse, concentrate on keeping your heels down and your legs tight against the horse's sides. Remember a good seat is necessary before you will ever acquire good hands. Without a firm seat you can never have effective hands. Think about this.

Continue with the slow trot, regardless of how many lessons it might take, until you are no longer tense and can truthfully say to yourself, "I am really 'with' my horse. I am not punishing his mouth by inadvertent yanks and I can keep my seat."

This acquisition and maintenance of a secure seat is essential as you progress in each stage of learning. Your sensitivity, or lack of it, to the horse and his responses will be an indication here of your ability and natural aptitude for equitation.

A good exercise to improve your balance is to drop your stirrups and sit to the slow trot without them. However, don't attempt this exercise until you are confident that you can stay in the saddle without relying on the reins to hold you there! It is a good exercise but *you will know* when you are ready for it. At first, don't do this for too long a period as you will quickly get tired and begin to defeat yourself by clutching the mane and hanging on to the horse's mouth. Use good judgment.

POSTING

Assuming that you have now managed to retain your seat successfully while keeping your horse in his slow trot, you must next learn to post. If you have performed the sitting trot to your satisfaction—both with and without stirrups— you will find that, once learned, the posting trot will be easier and less tiring for you.

Posting means that you will rise from your saddle so that you catch the gait's rhythm, and come back to the saddle at every other hoofbeat. The horse's gait, a steady, not-too-fast trot will help to lift you from the saddle once you have caught the cadence of his hoofbeats. It takes time and practice but soon you will learn to rise and fall automatically with his motion.

Trotting without
Stirrups

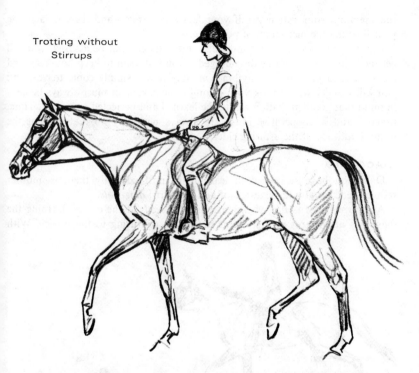

With your weight in your heels—which *must* be kept down, down, down—keep your knees supple while lifting yourself off them. In other words: don't work too hard. Let the horse's motion push you from the saddle and return to it as lightly as you can. So many beginners, when learning, thrust their bodies violently into the air, trying to catch the motion of the horse. Relax. Let the horse do the work. Try to catch the rhythm of his gait without making a production of it. When you begin to feel that you are catching on, incline your body just *slightly* forward but keep your back from rounding. Don't hunch over. It is most important that you stay with the horse's motion and not let your legs get out ahead of you. If this happens, you will be behind the horse's motion and feel awkward and out of balance. Keep your legs back behind your knees with your heels down and your weight in them. You will find that you can maintain your seat better if your legs are correct—and thereby facilitate your learning the mechanics of posting.

Learning to post, like everything else, takes time. But be assured, you will get the hang of it. Don't be discouraged if you just seem to keep bouncing and can't seem to pick up the rhythm. One day it will simply come to you and you will wonder why it took you so long to achieve it. It must always be kept in mind that good equitation cannot be learned and perfected overnight. Time, practice and a cooperative horse are always necessary no matter what the natural aptitude of the aspiring rider.

DIAGONALS

Once you have succeeded in learning to post correctly there is another requirement for you to be aware of and to learn: *diagonals*.

As you will learn later when mastering the *leads* at the canter, learning the diagonals at the trot at first seems dreadfully confusing to the novice. With

Right Diagonal

Left Diagonal

both leads and diagonals, it is best and makes it easier for the beginner to comprehend, if he stands and watches an experienced rider perform and explain, at each change of diagonal, the "how" and "why" of it. Now, while the lead is performed by the *horse*, the diagonal is performed by the *rider*.

The use of the diagonals is shown in the illustrations.

Although they are most important when riding in a ring or in a circle, it is still necessary that the beginner learn what diagonals are and how to take one or the other whenever he wishes or on command.

Watching the rider trotting his horse in a counterclockwise direction, you will notice that when the horse extends his right leg (the one nearest the rail) the rider is out of the saddle, i.e. rising in his stirrups. When the horse's left, or inside, leg is extended he is back in the saddle. Each time he rises, or posts, to the trot in this direction the horse's right leg is extended. He is therefore on the *right diagonal*. When the rider reverses his horse, trotting in the clockwise direction he is correctly posting on the *left diagonal*; he is rising from the saddle as the horse extends his left leg and sitting when the right leg is down.

When you have watched a while and seen how the diagonals appear from the ground and think you have a clear idea of how they work, mount your horse and try it yourself.

Going counterclockwise, put your horse into a trot, sitting to it until you get your correct position and the rhythm of the gait. Watch his shoulders closely and when you see his right shoulder extend ahead of the other one, start posting. If your timing is good, you will rise from the saddle as the right shoulder and leg extend. Now, don't worry if you don't "catch" it the first time. If you see that you are wrong, sit your saddle and, when the right leg and shoulder extend again, rise from the saddle. You will get the knack of it easily if you understand what you are trying to do.

Most beginners have trouble with diagonals mainly because they do not *clearly* understand what is required of them. If you are a bit fuzzy on it, watch other riders till you thoroughly comprehend. Meanwhile keep practicing yourself. Remember: the right diagonal: counterclockwise direction, *right* leg extended and you are *up* from the saddle—left diagonal: clockwise direction, *left* leg extended and you are *up* from the saddle.

While you are practicing posting, practice your diagonals as well. It is a good exercise and excellent discipline.

Learning to post and learning your correct diagonals requires both practice and concentration so don't lose patience if you can't seem to get the hang of it at first. You will. Study the illustrations carefully.

THE CANTER

The canter is a collected gait; the horse is relaxed and in hand. For the beginner, it is best performed in a ring for two reasons: to facilitate putting the horse into his correct leads and for the security of the rider. In the canter, the horse "leads" with the legs (front and rear) on one side or the other.

Before you begin cantering your horse, it is important that you understand the meaning of the leads. Again, if possible, watch an experienced rider working his horse on both leads. Have him put his horse first on the left lead, then reverse direction and put his horse on the right lead. Notice the aids he gives his

Right Lead

Left Lead

ILLUSTRATED HORSEBACK RIDING FOR BEGINNERS

horse to put him on the correct lead. The illustrations show how the horse appears on either lead. Study them.

Now try your luck. With your horse at a walk, you have decided to put him on the left lead first. You will be going along the rail in a counterclockwise direction. Your first signal to the horse is to collect him by taking a slightly shorter hold on the reins. By collecting him this way, you will be not only getting his attention but will have him in balance to begin the next gait. When you feel him respond, waiting for your next command, take up slightly on the right rein, thus turning his head slightly outward. At the same time squeeze with your right leg. Also push with the left hip and back.

A horse will usually break into a canter from a walk if these aids are given with conviction. If he does not go right into his canter but begins to move off at a trot instead, stop him immediately and start again. A horse will soon fall into bad habits about his canter if allowed to "get away" with going into a trot first. He will become extremely sloppy about it, if he thinks he can get away with it! Be decisive. Be firm.

Sometimes, of course, it takes a beginner a few times before he is definite in his aids to his horse so that the horse understands what is being asked of him. Just be aware of the fact that your horse should not be allowed always to go into his canter "any which way."

Many beginners seem to have great difficulty giving the aids to canter to a horse. Either they are too timid or apprehensive and therefore are quite inept or they are too aggressive and thump and pound on the horse, confusing the animal completely. Many lack the coordination themselves to give a horse the aids he will understand. A horse is a creature of habit. If he has been taught to perform to certain definite signals; unless those exact signals are given, he becomes easily bewildered and will trot when he should canter or he will stand in place and teeter up and down, waiting for the correct aid to be given. Always be decisive and *consistent* when asking your horse for a canter.

Having succeeded in putting your horse into the canter, keep your legs in position and keep them as quiet as you can and hold your hands low. Sit down in your saddle, pushing your weight into your heels again. Your body should be just slightly inclined forward with your back straight but supple. Visualize, as your horse moves, the form of the rider in the illustrations. Try to emulate the image in your mind as you canter around the ring.

Left Lead

Right Lead

At first you will probably feel awkward, having difficulty keeping your seat in contact with the saddle. But if you will persevere in keeping your heels down and your weight thrust into them while not leaning too far forward with your body, you will gradually feel more relaxed and in balance with your horse. As with the other requirements, it takes time and practice. Never think otherwise.

Remember, try not to interfere with your horse. Don't bang him with your legs or snatch his mouth with the reins. If you feel yourself becoming out of balance, bring your horse back to a walk, relax and start again.

To canter him on the right lead, reverse direction and, following the same procedure, turn his head slightly to the left and nudge him with your left heel.

You will soon acquire the coordination to put your horse into his canter, recognizing immediately whether or not he is on the correct lead. With time, you will be able to "feel" a horse take the wrong lead even without looking down at his shoulder, thus being able to correct him at once if he goes off wrong.

CHECK YOUR PROGRESS

As you begin to feel yourself becoming at home at the three gaits described, begin to concentrate on improving your form and seat as well as management of your horse. Are your hands sensitive to the horse's mouth, feeling his responses through the reins? Can you pick up your correct diagonal at the trot without undue difficulty? Does your horse take either lead you ask him for on command and does he canter smoothly without pulling or breaking his gait? Do you feel as though you have a secure seat and can keep your legs in a reasonably good position? If you can answer "yes" to these questions you are progressing very well. If any of the answers are "no," then more work is required in that particular area. Sometimes having an experienced rider show you a certain point will make it seem less confusing to you. Leads and diagonals have discouraged many a beginner, so don't become exasperated if you sometimes think that you will never get them right. And if you feel that your form needs attention, a few lessons with a good riding instructor will be most beneficial, particularly if you ultimately plan to show in equitation classes.

The importance of your early training cannot be overstressed. It is far better to learn correctly from the start than having to break well-established bad habits later on.

THE HAND GALLOP

From the canter, you will next learn to put your horse into the hand gallop. This is merely a faster version of the canter. It is quite different from the all-out running of the Thoroughbred race horse on the track. It is, as its name implies, a gallop with the horse in hand: that is, collected and completely controlled and in balance. The horse merely extends his canter, picking up speed but remaining entirely in hand.

Your position in the saddle in the hand gallop changes only in that you incline your body farther forward and take a shorter hold on your reins. You will feel your horse extend himself as you urge him with your legs into the faster gait. But keep him back if he tries to surge forward too fast or too strongly and keep his pace steady and even.

You will probably find that maintaining your position in the saddle will tire you quite rapidly at first. Your back muscles, especially, will feel the strain as

The Hand Gallop

you keep your body inclined forward. Therefore don't gallop him too long at a stretch until your muscles become accustomed to the forward position.

To bring your horse back from the gallop, straighten your body and throw your weight back into the seat of your saddle. Take back on your reins at the same time until you feel your horse give in to you. Then ease up on the hold you have on his mouth as he breaks back into a trot and, finally, a walk. A pat on the neck will reward him for his obedience.

USE OF TACK

You have been riding your horse in a snaffle bridle to start and it is perfectly satisfactory to continue with it if he goes well in it. However, as part of your riding education you should also learn to ride with double reins.

When you feel you are riding well enough with the snaffle, it is time you tried using a Pelham bridle on your horse. The illustrations show two styles of Pelham bits which are popular: the rubber mouth and the plain mouth. Both come with different length shanks and various heights of port. For a light-mouthed horse, many horsemen like the Tom Thumb Pelham, which has very short shanks.

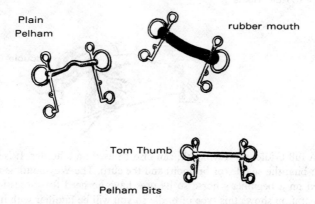

Plain
Pelham

rubber mouth

Tom Thumb

Pelham Bits

You bridle your horse the same way you did with the snaffle except for one more step: the fastening of the curb chain. Be sure the chain is smooth and not twisted and don't have it too tight.

The accepted way of holding double reins is shown in the illustrations. The hands are held at the same angle as with the single rein and the same distance apart. The top rein (the wider of the two) is held on the outside of the little finger while the bottom, narrower rein goes between the little finger and the fourth finger. As with the snaffle, light contact is kept with the horse's mouth but you will find, due to the action of the curb less pressure will be required to slow or stop a horse.

single

How to Hold Reins

double

A full bridle, or Weymouth, can also be used on a hunter. It is a bridle with two bits: the snaffle (or bridoon) and the curb. The Weymouth is not generally used on a beginner's horse so its uses have no need for discussion here. The illustration shows this type of bridle so you will be familiar with it, however.

The use of a riding crop or spurs is better left until you have mastered the fundamentals of equitation. Both can get you in trouble if improperly applied. We are assuming your horse is well-schooled for your basic work and will not need them, anyway! Later on, when you have got to the intermediate stage, you may wish to wear spurs when performing a bit more advanced work with him.

A WORD ABOUT JUMPING

Although for the beginner, jumping is rather a long way off, it is good to have some idea of the basics of it.

Cavaletti

Don't however, attempt any of this until you have established a secure seat at the walk, trot, canter and hand gallop and can truthfully say you have control of your horse completely.

You will begin to learn to jump your horse by the use of a series of rails or low obstacles. These are called, "cavaletti." At first they will be put in a line lying directly on the ground. And you will trot your horse over them, keeping your body in the position you used when hand galloping.

You should maintain light contact with your horse's mouth but don't interfere with his way of going as he approaches the rails. Keep him in hand and steady him only. With your body inclined forward, your weight down in your heels and your hands forward of the horse's withers, you trot over the cavaletti, keeping your position consistent all the while. Regardless of whether the horse hops over the rails or merely trots normally over them, endeavor to maintain your jumping position. If he should jump, be sure your hands are forward and flexible enough so you are able to give him his head and not catch him in the mouth unexpectedly. Over higher fences there is nothing that will sour a horse faster than having his rider get left behind (out of balance) and snatch his mouth. So always bear in mind that the horse must have complete freedom to extend his head and neck when he jumps and see that you are in the position to allow him this freedom of movement. The illustrations show this in the approach, the jump and the landing.

When you are ready to try jumping an actual fence, keep it *low*. Overconfidence can be harmful at this point sometimes.

You may approach the low obstacle at a collected canter. Keep your head up and concentrate on keeping your position in the saddle. Your hands are still on the horse's neck, but don't attempt to signal the horse to jump. Let him rate himself at this point. As you feel him gather himself to take off, get up out of the saddle with your body inclined forward and your weight still in your heels. As he comes down your first tendency will be to flop forward. This can be avoided if your knees hold you securely in the saddle and take the shock of the landing. Don't loosen up so that you lose control of your position.

Remember to try to avoid being "left behind." This happens when you are not in the proper position and are thus out of balance, so that when the horse leaves the ground you are unable to stay with him. Getting left behind is rough on both rider *and* horse for reasons which are obvious. Study the illustration showing this problem.

Riders Being Left Behind

As you put your horse over successive low obstacles always concentrate on achieving that secure seat. With this will come responsive hands. Make no attempt to raise the height of the fences until you can consistently maintain your form and not interfere with your horse at any phase of the jump. Again, practice, practice, always bearing in mind the rules of the game. If, in mid-air, you feel you are going to be left behind, get your hands forward as much as you can so that you will not punish your horse's mouth. He can take your body flopping about up there far better than he can a nasty yank in the mouth.

With practice you will learn to anticipate how and when your horse will take off and be able to rate him accordingly. You will learn to urge him should he indicate a refusal or check him if his speed is not just right. However, all this is simply a matter of experience once the fundamentals are learned.

5. Riding Stock Seat

Assuming that you have already scurried around awhile looking at horses and have finally selected a suitable mount for your introduction to western riding, we will commence with bridling and saddling him.

BRIDLING

You will bridle the horse in the same manner as for the hunt seat. Study the illustration and apply the same principle to your western bridle. You will not have a cavesson to fasten, but you will have a curb strap on your western bit. This should be just loose enough to allow for two fingers to go between it and the horse's lower jaw. Adjust the bridle so that the bit comes to the corners of the horse's mouth, as shown.

Bridling Stock Horse

SADDLING

When saddling your western horse, you will *always* use a saddle blanket: either a single or a double (folded in half) depending on the horse's conformation. If he has extremely high withers, better use a double blanket. At any rate, allow for plenty of clearance between the pommel of the saddle and the horse's withers or you will be in trouble. When putting the blanket on the horse, place it slightly ahead of the withers and slide it *back* into place, in the direction of the hair, so that everything is smooth.

Flip the right stirrup and the cinches over the seat of the saddle before swinging the saddle up onto the horse's back. Don't plop it down heavily; instead, ease it on and make sure it "sets" right by shifting around a bit until it seems to fall into place: not too far forward or too far back. It is a good idea then to go around to the other side and check to see if all the straps and cinches are hanging down correctly and are not caught under the saddle or twisted. This done, come around and do up first the front cinch then the flank cinch (if your saddle has one). The front cinch should be drawn up quite snugly to keep the saddle firmly in place. However, the flank cinch (used mainly for roping) should be just tight enough to barely touch the horse's belly. It should *not* hang loose, as

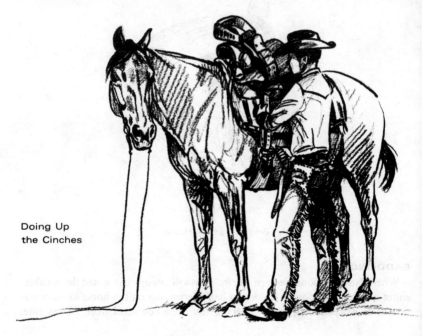

Doing Up
the Cinches

78

the horse, when kicking at a fly, could easily get "hung up" in a floppy cinch. Since, as explained in the case of the hunter, a wise old horse usually "blows up" when the cinches are tightened, take a couple of steps with him and then tighten your straps again. If you don't, you might find the saddle turning with you when you place your weight in the stirrup.

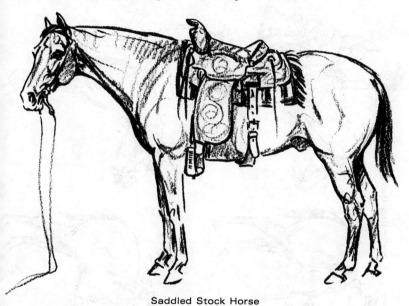

Saddled Stock Horse

MOUNTING

In preparing to mount, stand beside your horse on the near side. Although there are several schools of thought about the direction to face when mounting the stock horse, most generally accepted is the one that says, face the saddle squarely. With your reins in your left hand, place that hand on the horse's withers. Keep light contact with the horse's mouth to keep him standing still when you mount. Don't pull him, though, or he is apt to back as you swing into the saddle. Now grasp the stirrup with your right hand and, after putting your left foot into it, take hold of the saddle horn or the cantle with your right

Mounting the Stock Horse

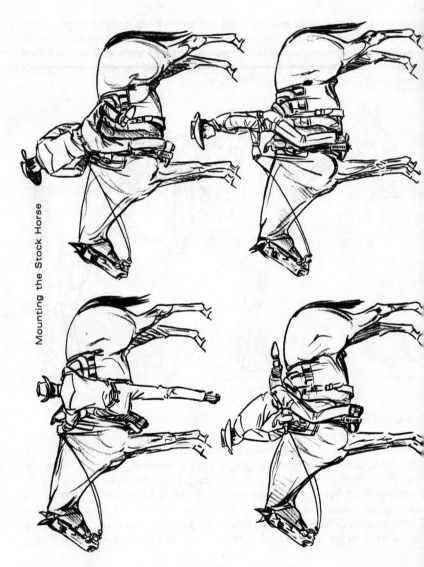

hand and lift yourself up onto your left stirrup. As you swing your right leg over the horse's croup, avoid bumping him with your toe. Ease yourself into the saddle lightly; don't come down with a bump: it is neither correct nor attractive to flop down into the saddle like a bag of grain. Take your right stirrup and check to see if they are both the same length.

Practice mounting and dismounting, so you can do it with some finesse at the outset. To dismount, keep your reins in contact with the horse's mouth and dropping your right stirrup, swing your leg back over his croup again. Then with your left foot still in the stirrup, step down from the horse.

ACHIEVING A CORRECT SEAT

When you feel you have got the knack of mounting and dismounting, and are relaxed and assured that this first step has been mastered, mount your horse

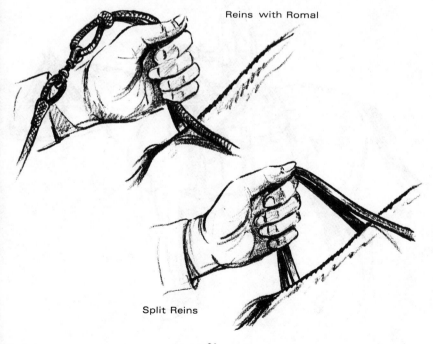

Reins with Romal

Split Reins

again with your reins held correctly in your left hand. If you have a romal on your reins, you will hold them, as shown, with your hand *around* the reins, the ends falling on the off side of the horse. With split reins hold them as shown in the illustration.

Your position in the saddle should be, first of all, comfortable to you. Be sure your stirrups are properly adjusted. If possible, because they are usually more difficult to adjust on a stock saddle, have someone help you.

To sit correctly, your back should be straight, but not rigid—and not tilted backward or forward. Your shoulders should be square, not turned one way more than the other to throw your balance off. Your knees should be slightly

Proper Stock Seat

bent with your heels lower than your toes. Your weight should be over the balls of your feet and your legs parallel with the horse's sides. Never thrust your lower legs straight to the outside or too far forward. These are common faults often seen among new riders. It is both unattractive and impractical. And don't slouch. This not only looks terrible, it becomes uncomfortable very soon. Your weight should not be too far back on the cantle of the saddle as you will then be out of balance with the horse.

Sitting in the middle of your horse's center of gravity with your legs under you and in contact with the horse's sides, you are in position to guide the animal not only with your reins but with your weight and legs as well.

Your reining arm (left) should be parallel with the horse's top line (back) and the elbow positioned so that your upper arm is vertical. You should be relaxed in mind and body. If you are tense you will inadvertently stiffen your body and your hands, thus defeating yourself at the start. Unless you are over-mounted (have a horse that is too much for you) there is certainly nothing to fear in learning to ride stock seat. On the contrary it is probably the simplest seat to learn to ride correctly!

THE WALK

With your position in the saddle as described above, put your horse into a walk. This is accomplished by lifting your rein hand slightly and contacting the horse's mouth to signal him. At the same time, squeeze him with your legs. If he moves out right away, these are all the aids you will need to get him started. If he is a bit sluggish about it, touch him with your heel and cluck to him until he moves off. Don't overdo the clucking, though; if it does not work right away, use your legs and heels more firmly.

Your left hand, holding the reins, should be just above the saddle horn; the right hand should rest naturally and comfortably on your right thigh. Never let your right hand flop about freely, as is often seen. This waving in the breeze of that free arm immediately identifies the inexperienced rider and looks terrible besides! If you feel as though you must do *something* with that hand, hold the hanging ends of the reins, but keep your hand low and still on your thigh as shown.

Walk your horse off, getting the feel of his motion and his reactions to the aids you give him. If he has been well-trained he will turn when you press the reins against his neck. This is known as neck-reining. As opposed to direct, or

The Walk

plow-reining, where the rein is pulled on the side of the direction you wish to turn, neck-reining operates on the principle that the horse moves *away* from the pressure of the rein on his neck. Therefore, if you wish your horse to turn to the left, you simply press the rein against the right side of his neck. If he has been trained properly, he will instantly move away from the rein and turn left. The same applies when turning to the right: rein against the left side of his neck. Keep your reining hand just above the saddle horn so your rein is horizontal when you turn your horse.

Since we are concerned with the fundamentals of riding, not horse training, we will not go into how the horse is taught to neck-rein here. Too much information all at once bogs down the mind of the beginner. We will just assume your horse is trained to neck-rein properly and let it go for now.

As you walk your horse, turn him occasionally first to the left and then back to the right in the manner described above. Do you understand the principles of neck-reining now? How does he respond for you? Does he keep his head down and his mouth quiet when you rein him each way? Or does he toss it, fighting the bit when you apply tension on the reins?

Continue to work your horse at a walk until you have the feel of his mouth and he is reacting correctly to your aids. As you make your turns, use your legs

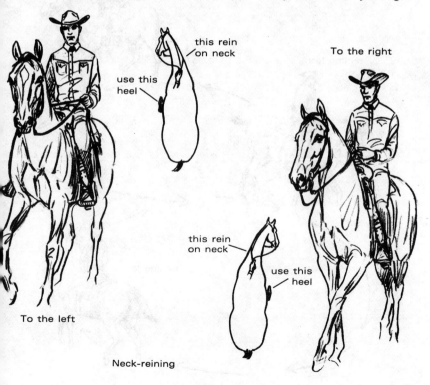

this rein on neck

use this heel

To the right

this rein on neck

use this heel

To the left

Neck-reining

too, as another aid. Remember that he will always move *away* from any applied pressure, whether it is your leg on his side or the rein on his neck.

Try walking him in a circle, reining him lightly as he comes around. Keep your reining hand low and the reins just short enough so you have full control without either too tight a hold *or* an overly loose and sloppy rein.

Figure 8 at a jog

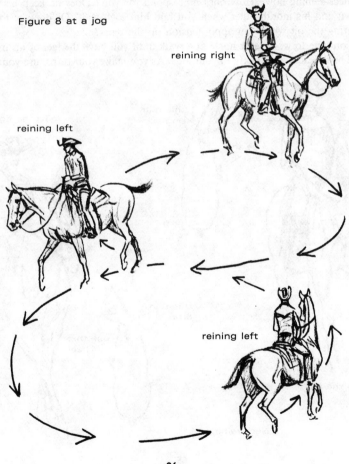

reining right

reining left

reining left

86

When you have him doing circles well, try doing figure eights with your horse. This exercise requires you to turn him in two directions: first to the left and then to the right. Do you feel "with" him as he makes his changes of direction? Can you see how the distribution of your weight in the saddle seems to aid him as he comes around?

These are questions to ask yourself as you perform these maneuvers at a walk. When you begin to loosen up and feel the horse responding to your commands, keep practicing the figures. There is no need to hurry on just yet. Hurrying usually leads to bad habits. Keeping your horse at a walk, you will gain confidence faster and the basic rules of guidance will become clearer to you. You will learn that, when you shift your weight in the saddle, the horse will respond accordingly, that he is sensitive to your balance and leg pressure as well as the rein.

Even if you keep your horse just walking for the first few sessions with him, you will have established a rapport with him which is invaluable to you as a rider. The maneuvers you perform with him at this gait will be easily accomplished and can hardly lead to any sort of accident which might shake your confidence at this important time. So keep him walking and turning to learn his reactions as well as your own.

THE JOG

When you feel you have gained confidence and have clearly understood your horse's responses to given aids, let him jog.

Keeping the same position you had at a walk, touch your horse with your heel, signaling him simultaneously with your reins by lifting your hand *slightly* (not forward), contacting his mouth with a light nick to get his attention. He will break into a jog with these aids. The gait should be, as its name suggests, slow and relaxed. And you should not let your body hunch forward when the horse increases his speed from the walk. Nor should you throw your weight too far back on the cantle, either. Try to remain in your saddle's center, letting your legs relax against the horse's sides. Keep your hands relatively low and don't let your reins get too loose and sloppy as you will not be able to control your horse well should he turn unexpectedly or be startled by something. Keep your rein hand in the position so that you can be with the horse at all times. A loose and floppy rein is just as bad as too tight a rein in some ways. At first you may find just keeping your seat is enough to worry about, but as you

The Jog

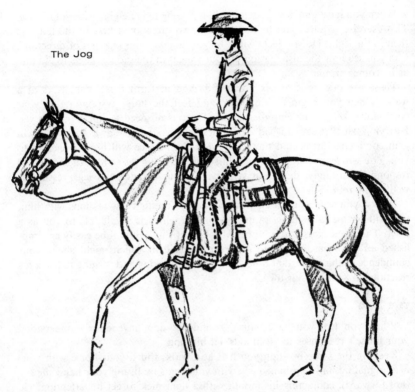

progress keep in mind that you must try to just feel your horse's mouth with the reins: no clamping on and no flopping!

It is important not to tense up any more than you can help it as this will only make the gait seem more difficult to sit to. If you maintain your correct position, you will soon find that you will become as confident jogging as you had become at the walk.

Ideally, you should be working your horse in some sort of riding ring or enclosure at the start, so you can keep him on the rail at the jog until you have gained confidence. Keep the gait very slow so you won't bounce about unduly until you have the hang of it.

As with the walk, try to get with the horse's motion. Push your weight into your seat, letting your knees absorb some of the motion, too. Most important is endeavoring to keep your correct position in the saddle, for if you lose this, everything will go wrong: your heels will come up, your reining hand will become ineffective and you will find yourself completely out of balance with your horse. Remember: heels down, shoulders square, legs relaxed *against* the horse's sides, reining hand low and just over the horn (if your arms are extremely long, just in front of the saddle horn), head up. Let your horse move along the rail slowly as you work on, sticking tight to that saddle at an easy jog.

Until you feel you have accomplished the jog reasonably well: the time depends on your individual ability—stay at the rail and work on correcting and maintaining your seat. Rein your horse only as often as needed to keep on the rail and concentrate on sitting down in the saddle. As you improve, try to keep your rein hand as quiet as you can. The horse will travel steadier for you if you do not interfere with his mouth unduly.

Alternate between a walk and jog until you begin to feel relaxed and at home at both gaits and can maintain your position in the transition between the two. Practice, practice: when you know the fundamentals time and practice alone will increase your prowess.

The same maneuvers—circles, figure eights and serpentines can be performed as soon as you feel you have enough control of your horse to do them. But don't hurry. Don't venture from riding the rail until you honestly feel that you will not tense up should your horse miss a cue or take a few liberties with you. Don't let bravado make you tackle something you are not quite ready for!

When the time comes that you understand your aids—and how your horse is likely to respond to them—and you think you are able to put him through the various figures safely, then perform in the same manner as you did at a walk. But keep your jog slow and collected. And keep light contact with your horse's mouth, feeling him through each turn. Being in balance with him at all times is highly important. If you attempt excessive reining before you are ready, you take the chance of spoiling your horse by confusing him with indistinct aids or inadvertent cues. Be determined and be thorough in your demands upon yourself as well as upon your horse. You will be a better rider for it.

Once a bit of confidence is gained, the beginner often lets himself take chances which put his future confidence in jeopardy. We find this particularly true in the stock seat beginner. That "ole saddle horn" to hang on to, if the going gets rough, increases the sense of security and consequently chances are taken which can lead to trouble.

So keep your horse at a walk and a jog until you are completely relaxed and in harmony with him.

THE LOPE

With practice, now, we will assume that you have achieved a reasonable seat and feel very much at home in the saddle. You have learned to guide your horse well with both the reins and your legs. His responses to given aids understood, he is working well for you at the walk and jog and performing turns and

The Lope

transitions from the gaits smoothly. You are beginning really to communicate with him, knowing how much pressure on the bit will regulate his speed. Your legs are relaxed and comfortable, with your heels consistently down. You have learned that it is not necessary to tug at his mouth to stop him, nor wrench him around with the reins to make your turns. If your horse has been well-trained and has an even disposition (to tolerate the fumblings of the beginner) he will teach you while you are teaching yourself. Working together carefully and consistently, you and your horse by now are beginning to respond to each other. Not hurrying has paid off—in the confidence and enthusiasm you now have.

If you begin with a crash program toward learning to ride stock seat, rushing into every phase too rapidly, you may either get hurt through negligence or fail to acquire a good basic seat.

If you have ever watched a top professional western rider, you will have noted how quietly and smoothly he works his horse. There is no bravado displayed by the real expert. His horse functions with no apparent aids from the rider. His reining hand is low and flexible and he seems indeed to be a part of his horse. This is stock seat equitation as it should be, not as we see it on the screen. This is a point to ponder.

The first and most important consideration before putting your horse into the lope is an understanding of the leads. What is meant by the correct or incorrect lead? The experienced rider always knows instantly whether or not his horse is on the correct lead and it is important for the beginner to learn to distinguish between them at the start.

From the illustrations you will see that, when loping in a circle, a horse should lead with his inside leg. The illustrations show first a horse on the left lead and then a horse on the right lead.

When the horse starts his lope going, say, counterclockwise, he should be leading with his *left* leg.

To achieve this, collect your horse to get his attention, turn his head slightly to the *right* and touch him with your right heel, nicking him lightly with the bit as you lift his head. A well-trained horse will usually break into the lope on the left lead when these aids are given. If he seems to lunge forward with too much acceleration, take him back on the reins until you feel him give in and come back to you. When he does, slacken your hold and give in to him slightly. He should settle down to a slow lope. Keep your rein hand low and,

Left Lead—Reining Left

if possible, your contact with his mouth light. If he is relaxed and loping easily without pulling, you are doing everything right! Now with him loping, concentrate on keeping your seat down in the saddle. Don't let your heels come up. This will ruin your balance and you may find yourself pitching forward and tensing up, thus defeating yourself completely. Push your heels down and, gripping firmly with your legs (they must not swing back and forth), try to maintain the tight seat and straight back which you had while walking and jogging. Relax. The lope is quite conducive to it.

Don't let your left hand ever get too high, for lifting the reins often signals a horse to increase his speed, especially when combined with an excessively loose rein. If you keep your hand low, you can more easily take him back should he pick up speed. But at all costs, don't lose your "cool"!

It is best for your initial time at a lope that you ride your horse in some sort of ring or enclosure. There are two reasons for this: 1, working on a rail will facilitate putting your horse on the correct lead and 2, should he misinterpret your aids and misbehave, he can't run off with you. He will also have a tendency to work more collectedly in an enclosure than out in the open.

Don't lope your horse for too long a time when starting out. If you get tired and feel yourself losing control, rein your horse back to a walk at once. When you have caught your breath, begin again. Your horse should be kept loping as slowly as possible both for his own training as well as yours. A slow, comfortable and relaxed lope is the hallmark of the stock horse and it will give you a smoother ride thus enabling you to relax yourself and stay "with" your horse more easily. Actually, the lope is the most satisfying of gaits once you have overcome any tenseness you may have. Ride with it; feel your horse moving evenly under you. Soon you will wonder why you were ever apprehensive at all.

Reverse your horse when you have successfully put him into his lope several times in the counterclockwise direction. Now try him on the right lead in the

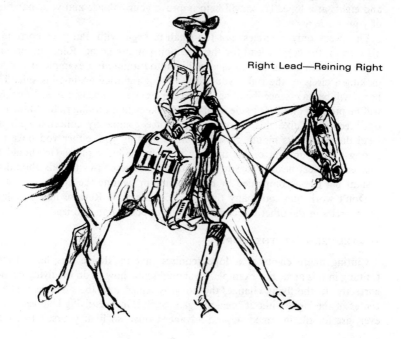

Right Lead—Reining Right

clockwise direction. This is achieved in the same manner as the left lead except that you turn your horse's head to the *left* and touch him with your *left* heel. The illustrations show how to identify each lead. From his *shoulder* you can see which lead he is on. When you have become expert, almost all you will have to do is glance at his shoulder or even just "feel" whether or not he has taken the correct lead.

Each time you ride, put your horse through his three gaits in both directions. This is very important, as the horse should be conditioned to working on both leads not just on one all the time. Always work on that seat so that you scarcely bounce at all at a jog and stick like glue at a lope. Keep a firm but supple grip with your knees—but remember, the key word in any form of riding is: relax. Enjoy it. Don't let it become a chore. Try to follow the rules but certainly strive to have *fun* while learning.

As your proficiency increases, you may wish to try a few of the simple circles and eights at a lope. These will help improve your balance and your handling of your horse as well.

First work only in circles: not too small to begin with. Put your horse into his lope on the correct lead for the direction you are going. Rein him around in the circle using your legs to squeeze him into turning. For example, if you are making a circle to the right, you will use your right leg against his side. The horse will be, in essence, bending *around* the leg pressure as he turns. Your rein will be pressing on the *left* side of his neck to keep him turning right. Make two or three circles like this, keeping your horse completely collected with his head down and his mouth closed. If he is fighting you, either you have too strong a hold on him or his training is faulty or incomplete. He should be relaxed and feel flexible to you as he turns. His responses to aids should be instant but not accompanied by head tossing or fighting the bit.

Don't work him too many times in one direction. Reverse him and lope your circles in the other direction using the opposite rein and leg.

MANEUVERS AT THE LOPE

Cutting figure eights at a lope requires that the horse has had special training in this area. For example, he should know how to do the flying change correctly. In the flying change, the horse is reined into the other lead at the center of the eight without breaking gait. Such things as flying changes, however, are for the intermediate and advanced rider, so limit yourself to circles

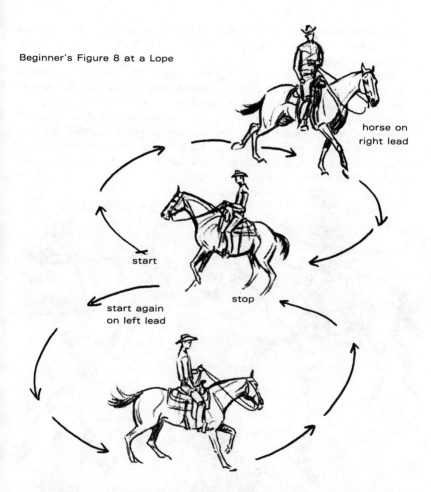

Beginner's Figure 8 at a Lope

horse on right lead

start

stop

start again on left lead

and simple changes of lead. If you must practice figure eights at this stage, do so by loping your horse in a circle, stop him at the center and then put him into his lope again in the opposite direction and the other lead. At first keep the circles fairly large but as your proficiency increases you may attempt tighter ones.

By doing these maneuvers you will see how important the coordinated use of your hands and legs will be to your horse's performance as well as to perfecting your balance and seat.

Practice your circles and eights, however, only to the point that your horse does not become bored with it all. It is easy to sour a horse with too much of this. Vary his activities to keep him interested and pleasant in his attitude.

Of course you will ride him on the trail, too, preferably in the company of experienced riders, once you feel you can manage him sufficiently. But here use your head. Don't attempt anything that is beyond your ability just because the others are doing it. It is better to decline that invitation to a race to "the top

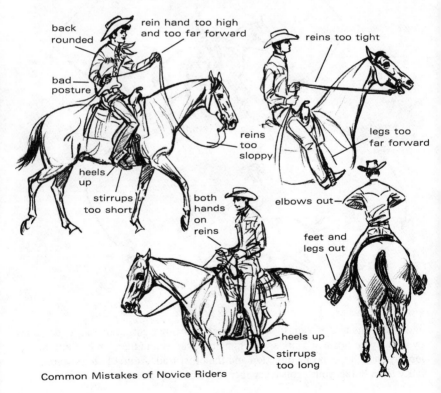

Common Mistakes of Novice Riders

o' the hill," than to walk back 10 miles because you and your horse parted company during some foolhardy escapade.

A FEW TIPS

Riding stock seat is one of the most satisfying ways of enjoying your pleasure horse. And when your equipment, your clothes and your riding are correct, it becomes all the more so.

It is not difficult to have everything in respect to your riding correct, both in appearance and from the angle of practicality. Rules to remember are:

1.—Make sure your saddle fits you and is completely comfortable (nothing is more agonizing than a stock saddle which makes you hurt somewhere!). If it isn't right for you, don't suffer: trade it for another that *is* comfortable or you'll become quickly discouraged by the whole thing. This is really important.

2.—Dress neatly. No matter whether you are wearing jeans, or expensive saddle pants, there is no excuse for being sloppy. Even on the trail neatness in dress gives *you* a lift and shows you take your riding seriously. Western riding used to have a bad name because so many of its devotees were careless of their appearance. With all the beautiful western fashions available today in all price ranges, there is no excuse for sloppiness in dress. Follow the trend!

3.—Remember *top* western riders are *quiet* riders generally. No matter what you might favor, the best performances are the smooth, collected ones where the horse is working willingly and in complete harmony with his rider. And when you are ready to go on to cutting and reining or showing, these rules will still apply.

6. Riding Saddle Seat

While almost any type of horse is suitable, or can be trained to be suitable, for the stock seat or hunt seat beginner, to learn to ride saddle seat well, ideally you should have a horse of the so-called "saddle type." In other words, you need a horse trained to the full bridle, who will give you the important "feel" of the show horse even at the start. This is not to say that you should rush right out and buy a top ring performer now, but that the horse you select should have the proper conformation if you are to learn how the saddle type differs from the hunter and the stock horse in his responses and way of going.

Though agreeable and well-mannered, he should be a "heads up" kind of horse who *thinks* rather like a show horse but whose fires have been banked, as it were! A lazy, low-headed "plug" would just not be suitable for this seat.

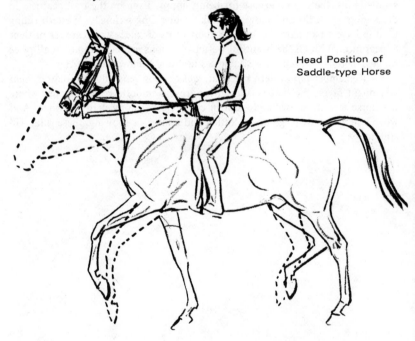

Head Position of
Saddle-type Horse

While the American Saddlebred horse was most responsible for the evolution of the saddle seat and, therefore, is probably the natural choice for the rider who chooses this style, the Morgan, too, is a very suitable mount for the beginner. He has the type and conformation and in the case of the Park Morgan, the action as well, to be an appropriate horse for the saddle seat rider. The requirements for the hunter are good bone and substance, while the saddle seat equitation horse must have style, quality and refinement, plus a generous amount of knee and hock action at the trot.

For the beginner, however, only the training and type is important. The horse you choose should, of course, have an even disposition and a good mouth.

BRIDLING

Since a beginner's hands as well as seat must be acquired in stages, we would suggest that the full bridle, correct on this type of horse, be put away at first. Less difficulty will be encountered if you begin by using the snaffle-martingale

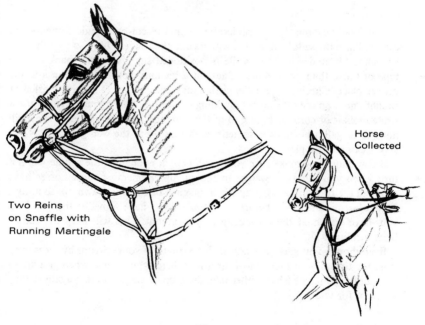

Horse
Collected

Two Reins
on Snaffle with
Running Martingale

arrangement shown here. A long-shanked curb, although correct, can be a lethal weapon in the hands of the beginner.

So it will be well if you tack your horse up in the snaffle bridle at first. You will use two reins on the bit: a snaffle (wider of the two) and a curb rein. The narrow curb rein is run through the reins of the running martingale while the snaffle reins (put on *above* the curb rein) is free. This will give you some of the action and "feel" of the full bridle without the extreme leverage of the show curb bit. Most well-trained Saddlebred Horses and Morgans go quite well in this arrangement. Indeed, many professional trainers use it for training young horses or for exercising their show horses.

Study the illustrations to see how this is adjusted on the horse and bridle him in the manner shown for the hunt and western seats. The cavesson should be snug and the martingale straps short enough so that there will be a definite curb effect when the reins are shortened. In this way you will learn how to manipulate a curb *and* a snaffle without putting your horse's mouth in jeopardy.

SADDLING

Now, saddle your horse, preferably with the cut-back saddle mentioned earlier. Place the saddle up on the withers and then slide it back so that the hair lies smoothly under it. The saddle is positioned slightly farther back on this type of horse than on a hunter. Shake it a bit until you feel it settle into the proper place. Check to see if the girth straps and the billets are not twisted or caught under on the off side before doing up your girth. You may wish to use a white mohair or cord girth instead of the web girth for everyday use. They will not rub or gall a horse as is sometimes the case with the web girth if it is not kept clean and supple.

Before mounting make sure your girth is tight enough so the saddle will not turn when you put your weight in the stirrup. Remember most horses have acquired the trick of blowing up when the girth or cinch is drawn up, so always have a last minute check before mounting. If you have someone there to help you, have him hold the off stirrup as you mount. This will keep the saddle from turning it all.

Even though you may have adjusted the length of your stirrups by measuring from the tips of your fingers to your armpit before mounting, when you are in the saddle you may wish to either take them up or lengthen them again so they are right for you.

Position of Cut-Back Saddle

MOUNTING

You mount in the same basic manner as shown in the other styles of riding. However, you may wish to put your horse in a stretched or "park" position before mounting. Most trained Saddlebreds and many Morgans will take this position automatically when they are standing still. To signal a trained horse to do this, you simply touch him on the near elbow, giving a little lift forward on the reins. Most horses will immediately square themselves up and assume the stretched position. An advantage to this is that a horse trained in this manner is less likely to move forward when you mount, as he has been taught to stand *still* when he is in the park position.

Swing up into your saddle after having placed your left foot into the stirrup. As you bring your right leg over the horse's croup, avoid bumping him with your foot. Come down as lightly as you can into the saddle.

101

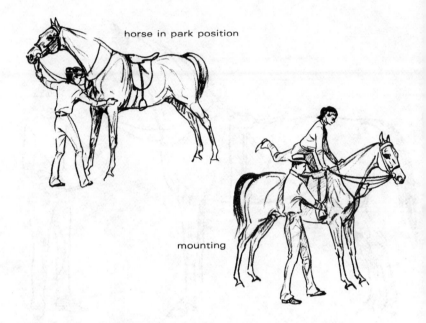

horse in park position

mounting

ACHIEVING A CORRECT SEAT

Your position should be as shown in the illustration. Since the saddle differs greatly in style from the forward seat jumping saddle, your position in it is likewise quite different. The cut-back style you ride is designed for a horse with naturally high head carriage. You will notice as you look down from the saddle that the horse's withers are not covered by the pommel of the saddle but that the withers and neck seem to rise out of the cut-back portion of the pommel. With a high-headed, high-necked horse, a saddle without the cut-out portion would have a tendency to interfere with the action of the horse's neck. The illustration show why the cut-back saddle is best on this type of horse.

Now that you are mounted and are comfortably positioned and adjusted, take your reins in both hands, using the double reins as though they were on the full bridle. With your hands at about a 45° angle, hold the wider rein, the snaffle, around the little finger and the curb rein between the little and the fourth finger. Use your thumb to hold them down.

As you prepare to move your horse out, ask yourself if your stirrups feel right to you. If they do not, a good way to readjust them is to take your feet out and let them hang loosely against the horse's sides. Then bend your knees slightly, take your stirrups again and adjust the leathers. The angle should not be as acute as in the hunt seat but the stirrups should not be so long that you will feel insecure and not be able to control your lower leg. Study the illustration of the correct position. You will see that the rider seems to be sitting farther back in the saddle than the hunt seat rider. The reason for this is that the seat must conform to the type of horse being used.

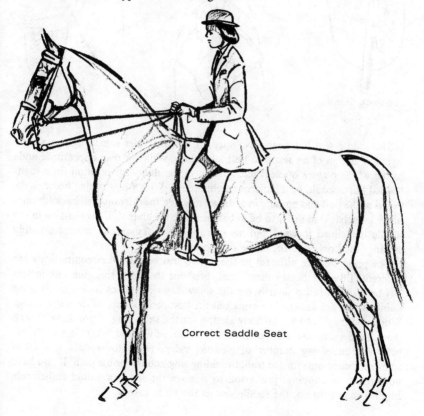

Correct Saddle Seat

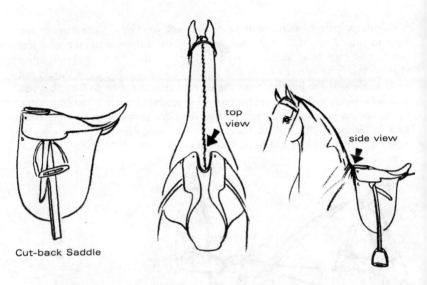

top
view

side view

Cut-back Saddle

The saddle seat has been developed so that the rider can bring out all the style and action of his horse to best advantage, while his own appearance adds to the whole picture of elegance. A rider in the hunt seat position on a high-headed horse would be a ludicrous sight indeed. With a big-fronted horse, well-flexed at the poll and moving in a showy manner, the rider must sit back (though not *leaning* back) in order to be in balance with the animal. If his position in the saddle is inclined forward and his stirrups are too short, he cannot possibly enhance the horse's performance or appearance.

The principles are different in the saddle seat because the requirements are different. Like the horses themselves, bred for the show ring, the saddle seat has been developed primarily for the show ring rider. Thus its emphasis is on points which are designed to bring out the best performance of the show horse. While you may not be ultimately aiming for the show ring, if you have chosen the saddle seat, you should understand the why's and wherefore's of this field. An increasing number of pleasure riders enjoy the saddle seat (with some modifications) for the trail, the riding ring and the bridle path. If you have no interest in jumping, preferring to ride on the flat, yet would rather ride English than western, the saddle seat is the ideal answer.

But we have digressed a bit and left you sitting up there with your stirrups hanging!

Adjust your stirrup leathers to the length that is right for you and see that you have good contact with your knees. Now, while in the hunt seat you gripped with the calves of your legs as well as with your knees, in the saddle seat your knees and thighs will do most of the gripping. Because of the greater length of stirrup you will not be able to grip with the calves in the same way as in the hunt seat. You will be riding much more on balance ·than on grip, so it is essential that you understand the importance of achieving the proper position at the start.

We will assume that you are learning to ride on a Saddlebred which is slightly "long in the tooth" and wise with the wisdom that comes only from careful training and years of experience in the ring and out of it. This horse will immediately show you why there *is* such a thing as a saddle seat: the reason for its existence.

As you sit on this horse, you notice that his neck is up ahead of you rather than beneath you as on a stock horse or hunter. This lofty carriage of the neck

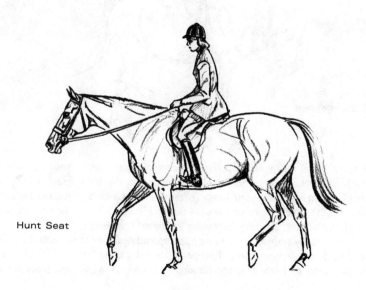

Hunt Seat

is one of the reasons for sitting back in your saddle. It would, as you can see, be completely wrong to incline your body forward on such a horse.

The correct position, therefore, is as shown, sitting back slightly in the saddle with your seat under you squarely (not protruding out behind you!), your back straight, your knees bent slightly with your heels—as always—*down*. Be sure your stirrups are not so long that you will be unable to keep your heels down. In all styles of riding, this is a universal rule: Keep those heels down. Your lower leg should be straight down or slightly behind your knee—*never* let it get out ahead of you!

Saddle Seat

When you feel that you are positioned correctly, take up on your reins; that is, gather your horse together by light pressure on the bit through the reins. Remember you are using your lower (narrow) rein as a curb so it must simulate the action of the curb. Since you always ride saddle seat with the horse collected, it is right to learn at the very beginning just what this means.

A Saddlebred is trained to carry its head up and flexed in at the poll. In order to keep his horse carrying himself properly, the rider must first "set" the horse's head and learn to keep it in the required position. A well-trained horse will respond easily to the action of the bits if they are correctly used. To avoid too much technicality at this point, we will state simply that the snaffle bit *lifts* the horse's head, while the curb *tucks in* his chin.

You will learn, as you progress, to work these reins (and bits) independently; but at this point, you should mainly be concerned with having your hands in the proper position and your reins held correctly. As a beginner, you are bound to fumble and feel at a loss sometimes, but with time and practice you will acquire proficiency and it will all seem much less complicated. There is every bit as much challenge in riding the saddle seat well and getting the performance from a show horse as there is in jumping a hunter over the highest fence or staying with the quickest-cutting stock horse!

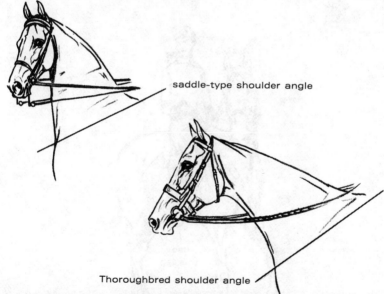

saddle-type shoulder angle

Thoroughbred shoulder angle

The head carriage of the saddle-type horse is always more erect than most other breeds, since the neck is set on the shoulder at an upright angle. The Thoroughbred, for example, has an equally good shoulder, but its neck is set on in front of his shoulder rather than on top of it.

THE WALK

To start your horse walking, press your legs against his sides behind the girth. Keep light contact, that is a light feel of the horse's mouth, as he moves off. You will see his head come up as he begins to walk. Now, if you can, gather him in on the lower (curb) rein. Can you feel him drop his nose and give in to it? A well-trained horse will do this, even in a snaffle-martingale arrangement, if properly cued. This is the reason a beginner should have a well-trained horse with which to start saddle seat equitation: so he can more easily grasp the basic requirements. An unresponsive horse can teach you nothing.

As your horse walks, keep your hands about four inches above his withers. Don't let your reins go slack but neither should you just clamp on to them with a "dead" pull either. Just try to feel his mouth lightly as he moves. It may seem difficult to comprehend at first, but on a Saddlebred the reins do much more

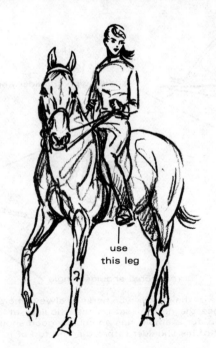

use
this leg

Turning Left

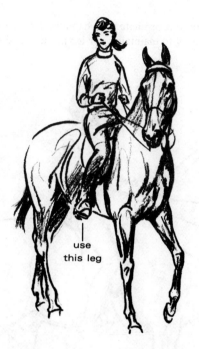

Turning Right

use
this leg

than just steer him. As you become more adept, you will find it becomes automatic to keep your horse's head in its proper position at all three gaits.

After you have walked your horse around the ring (you really *should* work in one) and have gained some understanding of the methods and their results, try turning your horse.

To turn your horse to the left at a walk, apply a bit more pressure on the left rein (you need only use your top rein here) and squeeze him with your left leg. He will move his body away from the leg pressure and turn in the direction of the rein pressure. As he reverses his direction, keep light pressure on the left rein, then use your right leg to get him going straight in the new direction. Remember a horse will always move *away* from any leg pressure.

Practice these turns until you see what makes him respond as he does. Never yank him around. Always keep your hands low and together when turning your horse and learn to coordinate your hands *and* legs in these turns. Practice at a walk, remembering to maintain your leg position and seat in the saddle as you work.

The Walk

THE TROT

After you have been walking and have begun to get the feel of setting your horse's head well and keeping it set and can keep *your* position, too, you will be ready to try a trot.

To put your horse into the trot, collect him as you did at a walk, squeezing him firmly with both legs. This will get him "up in the bridle" and he will work well under himself and be balanced. You will learn as you go along to feel how a trained horse correctly gathers himself together into a balanced trot rather than just shuffling off at a sloppy gait, all "apart" (disunited) and clumsy. It is up to the rider to see that his horse is set up and collected, so you will want to practice this.

The Trot

At first keep your horse at a slow trot, concentrating on keeping your seat correctly. If your hands do not seem to want to stay down and you cannot seem to get with the horse, remember that *all* beginners go through this no matter what seat they choose! Don't worry and get yourself all tensed up as a result. As long as you are familiar with the way things *should* be done and keep persevering, you will find that it all comes more easily to you each time you ride. Work at the slow sitting trot until you are not leaning forward and can keep your heels down and your legs where they belong. When you can sit the slow trot fairly well and keep your hands relatively still, you can begin the posting trot.

POSTING

The reason for posting is to make the normal trot easier and more comfortable for the rider. You must synchronize your actions with the motion of the horse. When posting saddle seat you use the same principles as in the hunt seat, but, of course, your position in the saddle is different. You are sitting with your body more erect and your stirrups longer. Therefore you may find that you have difficulty keeping your heels down. If so, shorten your stirrups just a little until you have learned to post.

Catching the up-down rhythm of the horse's gait is the basis of learning to post. As the horse moves at the trot, you will be thrown up out of the saddle by every stride the horse makes. The idea is to let the action of the horse lift you so that you rise and then sink back into the saddle in rhythm. As the horse trots, say to yourself, "up, down, up, down," until you have caught it. At first you will have some difficulty keeping from tipping forward as you try to catch the beat of the trot. This comes partly from being tense and partly from trying too hard.

To perfect your posting, do try not to work too hard at lifting yourself from the saddle. Let your horse do the work. His motion will push you up and if your knees are gripping lightly and kept springy, you will have to work very little to get out of the saddle while posting. So many beginners think they must push themselves frantically out of the saddle, twisting and contorting their bodies at each stride. This is neither necessary nor correct. Keep your legs in position, your knees supple and your body relaxed and you will soon find yourself moving *with* your horse and not as a separate entity. Working in complete unison with the horse is the goal; plenty of practice is the only way to achieve it.

Posting comes easily to some while others find it takes a bit longer to get the hang of it. Once you know how it should be done, simply keep working on it until you have mastered it. And you *will*!

DIAGONALS

Having attained this goal, you will next learn your *diagonals*. As with the hunt seat, the diagonals are an important exercise. Though they do not concern the western rider, who just sits to the jog (or slow trot), they are very much a part of your saddle seat education.

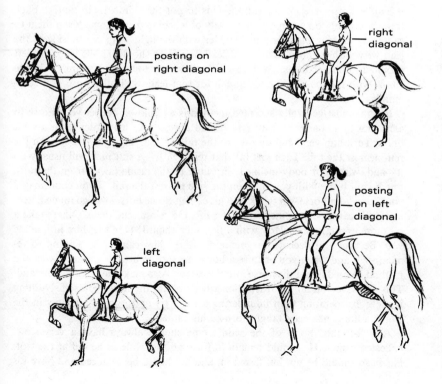

posting on right diagonal

right diagonal

left diagonal

posting on left diagonal

As mentioned earlier, there is a left and a right diagonal. When trotting your horse to the left in the ring, you should be posting on your *right* diagonal: that is, you should be out of the saddle as the horse extends his right leg. In the clockwise direction you will be on the *left* diagonal, posting when the horse's left leg is extended. If you don't catch the diagonal you want on the first try, bump your saddle once so you miss a beat, then come up as the horse extends the correct leg. Diagonals take a bit of practice, but they really are not difficult to learn if you understand clearly what should be done.

THE CANTER

Saddle horses are taught various aids to put them into their canter: Each trainer seeming to have his own pet way of teaching them. Some teach them to canter by tapping them on the shoulder with the light whip on the side of the lead they wish them to take: right lead, tap right shoulder; left lead, tap left shoulder. Another trainer will signal the horse by touching the animal in the elbow with the toe of his boot to call for that lead. Still others use oral commands.

But the most generally accepted method is as follows: collect your horse to alert him to a change of gait. (He should *always* take his canter from a walk only.) Turn him very slightly toward the rail by applying light pressure on the rein nearest the rail. Then just lift that rein lightly—a soft nick will usually do it—and, with your body inclined very little to the inside (away from the rail), touch your horse with your heel on the side nearest the rail. If you coordinated your cues, your horse will break into his canter. Some horses will go immediately into their canter the moment the rider lifts the rein to cue them. Others take a bit more urging; particularly with a beginner aboard! Don't let him intimidate you. Be firm and decisive in your aids. *Make* him canter! Something to remember if and when you acquire a horse, be sure to ask his former owner the method he used to put the horse into the canter. Also make sure you understand. This will save you untold frustration when you try the horse yourself. Nothing is more exasperating than floundering around trying to figure out how in the world a horse has been taught to take his canter!

A well-trained horse of the saddle type should always have a very slow, collected canter. He should remain in form all the while as he did at the trot. His head should be up, but flexed in, and he should be balanced and have his hocks working well in under himself. In other words, he should be completely in hand, with a precise, rocking-horse way of going.

If you should have difficulty putting your horse into the canter, or if he gets off wrong (takes the wrong lead), don't panic. Just stop him. Relax. Think over in your mind the instructions you were given to put him into it. Keep cool. And try again.

When you have him cantering and on the correct lead, and yet he seems to be overly strong, maybe he has got his head down and is leaning on the bit. In this case you will want to get him "off" the bit and carrying his head up again. If you can manage it, slack off a little on your lower (curb) rein and give him a couple of nicks with the top one. Don't just pull; this will not help at all. He will just fight you and you can't possibly beat him! Instead just keep nicking him lightly but without keeping a steady hold on his mouth. If you feel him

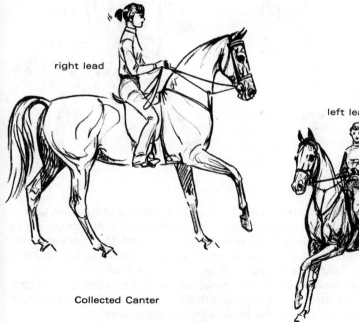

right lead

Collected Canter

left lead

giving in and his head coming back up, ease off and let him relax. He should lighten up in front and come back to you.

The Canter

As your horse canters, at first you may have difficulty sitting down tight to the saddle, and, instead, find yourself leaning forward out of balance. Try to keep your weight thrust down into your heels and push your seat under you, down into the saddle. Try also to keep your hands low, as to lift them may indicate to your horse that you wish him to move on faster.

Learning to coordinate is the most difficult part of learning to ride, but once you have mastered coordination and balance, you can move forward to refining your seat and educating your hands. Keep practicing. *Regularly.*

THE SLOW GAIT AND RACK

If you have purchased a Saddlebred that has been "gaited" at some time in his career, even though gaited horses are a bit beyond the beginner, you should know a bit about the two "man-made" gaits: the slow gait and the rack.

Both these artificial gaits are taught to a receptive horse by special training. The slow gait is a four-beat lateral gait where each foot hits the ground at a

The Slow Gait

different time. The rack is basically the same gait but performed at greater speed. When both are performed correctly, the horse has no tendency to pace. The pace is a two-beat gait and can be terribly uncomfortable to the rider and unattractive to the eye.

The illustrations show a horse at a slow gait and a rack so you can see exactly the mechanics of the gaits. Someday you will probably find yourself with a yen to show a gaited horse or a "walk-trot" as the three-gaited horse is called. It is exciting and great sport, too! However, until you have really mastered the saddle seat, it is best to leave the show horses to the experienced rider. But it's something to work for, isn't it?

USING THE SHOW BRIDLE

Because the full bridle or show bridle is correct for the Saddlebred or any horse that is ridden saddle seat, it is most important that you learn how it is correctly used.

The show bridle is actually two bridles in one: a snaffle and a curb. It is composed of two sets of cheek pieces and two bits. The leather straps throughout

Show Bridle

118

The Rack

are very narrow and neat-looking, being made of top quality fine leather. A fancy, colored browband is used and either a stitched cavesson or a colored one to match the browband. The reins, like the cheek pieces, are made of fine leather in the narrow width. The show bridle is designed to enhance the appearance of the fine-headed horse, as well as for utility.

You will bridle your horse the same way as before, except that with the show bridle you must hold both bits together and insert them into the horse's mouth carefully. Fastening up the bridle, the adjustments depend very much on the individual horse. Since your horse is (or should be!) well trained he probably will not need any special adjusting on his bridle.

With the bridle lengthened or shortened to fit the horse's head, the bits should rest comfortably in the horse's mouth. The curb bit should hang slightly lower than the snaffle which comes just to the corners of the horse's mouth. Fasten the throat latch just tight enough so that it doesn't flop about excessively nor be so tight that it interferes with the horse when he flexes in his head. Next, you fasten the cavesson strap, which buckles under the horse's lower jaw. This should be snug, *never* loose and flopping. Some horses may require a very tight cavesson to keep them from opening their mouths excessively. Lastly, the curb chain is done up. The degree of tightness depends entirely on the horse's mouth. But in general, the chain should be tight enough so that the curb bit does not have so much play in it that it must draw almost horizontal before it is effective. The illustration shows what is meant.

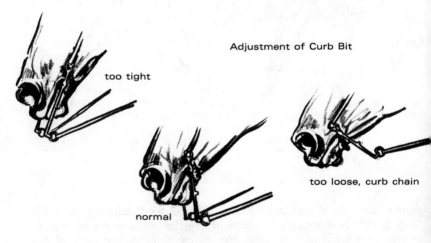

too tight

Adjustment of Curb Bit

normal

too loose, curb chain

Now with your horse thus bridled, you are ready to try your luck.

We will assume that by now you are quite familiar with the basics of the full bridle from your experience with the snaffle-martingale arrangement. So mount your horse, position yourself correctly and gather up your reins.

Using the same principle: snaffle rein around little finger, curb rein between little and fourth finger, you collect your horse by lifting his head with your snaffle and tucking him in with the curb.

Position of Hands for Collecting Horse

Before you move him off, check how he responds to the use of your fingers on the reins. Can you feel him drop his nose and flex in when you "tickle" his mouth with the curb? Does his head lift, yet remain flexed in when you nick him a couple of times with the snaffle? If you get these responses from him, both you and the horse are doing something right!

Now with his head and neck in their proper position, squeeze him with your legs and let him walk out. Let your hands give slightly with his motion, but keep his head where it belongs by light contact with his mouth. Walk him around

Light Contact

121

the ring, getting used to the feel of both bits. Your horse will probably be more responsive than he was in just the snaffle alone. When you lift him lightly on the snaffle, he should immediately elevate his head. If you feel his nose has crept out when his head came up, take up on the curb—not with a yank, but feeling his mouth with the bit. When he responds correctly, give in to him just a little to reward him. A well-trained horse will usually remain "set." As you walk, practice letting him relax and then pick him up and set him again.

Before you begin trotting, have a clear understanding of all this in your mind. You can be sure your horse will soon let you know how successful you have been!

standing   in action

Head Set

TROTTING WITH THE SHOW BRIDLE

To begin trotting, collect your horse as already shown. When he seems to be completely in hand, squeeze him with your legs, using them to urge him up even more into the bridle. If he feels light and airy in front, you know you have him set correctly. Keep him at a park trot (slow and stylish) posting lightly, with your knees springy and your body supple. Poise is very much a part of saddle seat equitation and acquiring it cannot begin too soon. With your horse performing precisely, you must endeavor to rival his form with your own.

Trotting with the Show Bridle

Both horse and rider must present a pleasing appearance as one unit. This is the goal for which to aim.

Even if you plan simply to ride saddle seat for pleasure, it is important for your own edification that you learn correctly both the requirements for your own form as well as the maintenance of the same in your horse. Your hands will be better for having gained the knowledge of how to collect a horse and bring out his best performance.

Since the trot is the Saddlebred's (and the Morgan's) most matchless gait, you will probably work hardest at perfection here. Remember the fundamentals discussed here: keep practicing; work always on the education of your hands as well as your seat. Learn to pick your horse up with the reins and coordinate this into collection by using your legs to urge him up into the bridle. Your horse, if he is indeed well trained, will teach you almost as well as any instructor how to be effective with the full bridle once you have learned the basic requirements for its use.

CANTERING WITH THE SHOW BRIDLE

There is no difference in cantering a horse in the full bridle except that it will take less effort to keep him slow and in form. Take your time putting him into it. Make sure you give him a clear aid. Keep your hands low and quiet as you ask him to canter. Take care not to catch him hard with the curb as he breaks into his gait. He is quite apt to thus throw his head and lunge into the canter. Give him the aid you have always used, gently but firmly. He should go right off into his correct lead. If he does not; ease him back and start again. (Never let a Saddlehorse go into his canter from a trot.) It is important to relax. Collect him again. Try giving him the mouth aid again with only the snaffle rein. Slack off a little on the curb rein. Perhaps you confused him with too much tension on both reins. Or if you were a bit uncertain or apprehensive, your horse probably sensed it and was confused when you asked him to canter.

When you have him cantering slowly and in form, keep light contact with his mouth even though he seems relaxed. Don't throw him away even if he is going easily. The reins should be just tight enough for this light contact. Never freeze on them. Keep your fingers limber and ready to give and take as he moves his head and neck.

Practice your canter on *both* leads, paying attention to your horse's reactions to the things you do. Ask yourself: does he keep his head up where it belongs while cantering? Or is he over-flexed and boring down on the bits? Are you thus lifting him with the snaffle with one or two nicks to get him to bring it up again?

If he will not get his head up despite your efforts, stop him and start again. This time make sure his head is up where it belongs when you begin to canter. You can keep it up, not by pulling on it but by just nicking him with the snaffle each time you feel him try to duck it down again. It is important not to let him continue this trick as it is easily developed into a very bad habit which is difficult to break.

As you go along you will find that being able to recognize the mistakes you see in your horse is part of learning; doing something about them is the test of your ability.

As time goes by and you become more and more adept at this riding style, not only will you find it very satisfying to be able to set your horse up correctly and have him performing letter-perfect for you but you will also enjoy yourself immensely in the process. It won't be long before you will be itching for a horse with a bit more "go" and style and be reading the horse show prize lists avidly.

As the hunt seat beginner yearns for the time when he'll be jumping Olympic-sized fences or hunting with a recognized pack, or the stock seat rider aspires to work top cutting horses; so most saddle seat riders aim toward the day when they will "win the Medal at the Garden" or ride to a Championship Tri-color on a brilliant show horse at an important event.

7. A Final Word

Whether you aspire to become a champion rider or are content to be merely a good rider (no mean accomplishment in itself), you will find that riding a horse is a serious discipline, but a rewarding one. The hours of practice required—and the practice is not all grinding labor, by any means—will be compensated later by hours of pleasure, enhanced by the knowledge that, whatever the style you choose to ride, you are performing correctly, with poise and assurance, in harmony with your horse; that you are, in effect, a horseman—a name that denotes both horse and rider, please note. Of the ever-increasing number of riders today, all too many are "park" riders—those who merely wish to cut a dashing figure, without proper preparation and often to the detriment of the horse. We need more horsemen. We hope that you will become one.

Index

age, 7
aids, 7, 59, 66, 83
American Saddlebred, 17, 19, 21, 23, 25, 42, 47, 48, 99, 100, 101, 105, 106, 108, 117, 118, 124
  five-gaited, 23, 117, 118
  three-gaited ("Walk-trot"), 23
Anglo-Arab, 22
Apaloosa, 9, 21, 24
Arabian, 16, 17, 18, 19, 20, 21, 22, 25, 45, 48
backing, 58–61
balance, 7
billets, 7, 100
bit, 7, 26, 27–28, 29, 37, 38, 43, 44–45, 49, 71, 107
  Pelham, 29, 71
  snaffle, 10, 43, 44, 72, 100
boots, 28–29, 30, 39, 45
breast collar, 37, 38
breeches, 30
bridle, 7, 26, 27–28, 29, 37, 38, 43, 44, 49, 62
  double-reined, 28, 71
  Pelham, 28, 29, 71
  snaffle, 43, 44, 49, 62, 71, 72, 99, 100, 108
  snaffle-martingale arrangement, 99, 108
  Weymouth, 28, 44, 71–72
bridling the horse, 49–51, 77, 99–100
bridoon, 45, 72
browband, 44
Canadian pacer, 23, 24
canter, 7, 14, 33, 56, 64, 66–69, 114–116, 124–125
cantle, 7, 27, 52
cavaletti, 73, 74
cavesson, 7, 44, 77
chaps, 39
choosing a horse
  hunt seat, 31–33
  saddle seat, 47–48
  stock seat, 39–42
chunk, 7, 31
cinches, 7, 36, 38, 78
circles, 86–87, 89, 94, 96
collecting, 7, 61, 67, 121
colt, 7
configuration of horse, 6
  faults, 34
correct seat, 55–56, 81–83, 102–107
crop, 72
croup, 7
curb, 7, 44, 71, 72, 100, 107, 108, 120
cut-back show saddle, 19, 42, 43, 100, 102, 104
dam, 7
"death grip," 60, 61
derby
  hard hunt, 28, 29
  hard saddle, 46

diagonals, 64–66, 69, 113–114
direct reining, 83–84
dismount, 52–54, 81
double-reined bridles, 28, 71
English tack, 11, 17, 18, 25, 26–30, 42–47
equitation, 7, 14
  terminology of, 11, 12
faults of configuration, 34
fender, 7
figure eights, 87, 89, 94, 95, 96
filly, 8
Fine Harness, 8, 23
five-gaited, 23, 117–118
flat, 14, 17
flying change, 95
foal, 8
forward seat saddle, 26–27, 55
gait, 8, 63
  collected, 66, 74
gaited horse, 8
gallop, 8
  hand, 70–71
gelding, 8, 41
girth, 8, 43, 50, 57, 100
grade horse, 8
hack, 8
hacking, 8
half-bred, 21, 22
hand, 8
hand gallop, 70–71
hands, 8, 14, 17, 59, 61
head shy, 8, 49
headstall, 37, 38
hock, 8
hunt seat, 11, 13–15, 18
  bridling, 49–51
  choosing a horse for, 31–33
  correct seat, 55–56, 61
  riding, 49–76
  saddling, 50–51
  tack and outfit, 26–30
hunter, 8, 20, 31
hunter hack, 8
irons, 8
jig, 8, 41, 57
jodhpurs, 30, 46
jog, 8, 87–90
jumper, 8
jumping, 73–76
leads, 64, 68, 69, 91–94
light horse breeds, 9
lope, 9, 41, 90–96
manners, 9
martingale, 9, 28, 44, 99, 108

martingale-snaffle arrangement, 99, 108
modified saddle seat, 19
Morgan, 16, 17, 18, 19, 21, 23, 24, 25, 42, 45, 48, 99, 100, 101, 124
mounting, 52, 79–81, 102
near side, 9, 49, 79
neck-reining, 83–85
off side, 9
pacer, 9
Palomino, 9, 21, 24
park horse, 9, 23
park position, 101
Pelham
    bit, 29, 71
    bridle, 28, 29, 71
    plain, 71
    rubber mouth, 71
    Tom Thumb, 71
Pinto, 9, 21, 24–25
plain Pelham, 71
pommel, 9, 78
port, 9
posting, 9, 62–64, 65, 112–113
purebred, 9
Quarter Horse, 16, 21, 22, 24, 25
rack, 9, 117–118, 119
registry, 9
reins, 9, 71
riding
    hunt seat, 49–76
    saddle seat, 98–125
    stock seat, 77–97
romal, 9, 38, 82
rubber mouth Pelham, 71
saddle, 26, 27, 35–36, 42–43, 55
    cut-back, 19, 42, 43, 100, 102, 104
saddle blanket, 38, 77
saddle horn, 9
saddle seat, 11, 17–19
    bridling, 99–100
    choosing a horse for, 47–48
    correct seat, 102–107
    riding, 98–125
    saddling, 100
    tack and outfit, 42–47

saddling, 50–51, 77–79, 100
seat, 10, 11
    correct, 55–56, 81–83, 102–107
serpentines, 89
signals, 67
sire, 10
slow-gait, 10, 117–118
snaffle
    bit, 10, 43, 44, 72, 100
    bridle, 43, 44, 49, 62, 71, 72, 99, 100, 108
    bridoon, 45, 72
snaffle-martingale, 99, 108
split reins, 82
spurs, 72
stallion, 10
star-gazer, 10, 31
stirrup, 10, 18
    adjustment, 50–52, 82, 100
stirrup irons, 43
stirrup leathers, 10, 43
stock, 10
stock seat, 11, 15–17
    bridling, 77
    choosing a horse for, 39–42
    correct seat, 81–83
    riding, 77–97
    saddling, 77–79
    tack and outfit, 33–39
tack, 10, 11, 26–30, 33–39, 42–47
Tennessee Walking Horse, 21, 24
Thoroughbred, 20, 21, 22, 23, 24, 31, 70
three-gaited, 17, 23
throat latch, 10, 49
Tom Thumb Pelham, 71
trot, 10, 14, 33, 56, 61–62, 67, 110–112, 122–124
turning, 57–58, 85–86, 109
walk, 10, 14, 56–61, 83–87, 108–110
walk-trot, 10, 23
western tack, 11, 25, 33–39
Weymouth bridle (full or show bridle), 28, 44.
withers, 10, 50, 52, 55, 78

A PERSONAL WORD FROM MELVIN POWERS
PUBLISHER, WILSHIRE BOOK COMPANY

Dear Friend:

My goal is to publish interesting, informative, and inspirational books. You can help me accomplish this by answering the following questions, either by phone or by mail. Or, if convenient for you, I would welcome the opportunity to visit with you in my office and hear your comments in person.

Did you enjoy reading this book? Why?

Would you enjoy reading another similar book?

What idea in the book impressed you the most?

If applicable to your situation, have you incorporated this idea in your daily life?

Is there a chapter that could serve as a theme for an entire book? Please explain.

If you have an idea for a book, I would welcome discussing it with you. If you already have one in progress, write or call me concerning possible publication. I can be reached at (213) 875-1711 or (213) 983-1105.

Sincerely yours,

MELVIN POWERS

12015 Sherman Road
North Hollywood, California 91605

ELVIN POWERS SELF-IMPROVEMENT LIBRARY

ASTROLOGY

___ ASTROLOGY: HOW TO CHART YOUR HOROSCOPE *Max Heindel*	3.00
___ ASTROLOGY: YOUR PERSONAL SUN-SIGN GUIDE *Beatrice Ryder*	3.00
___ ASTROLOGY FOR EVERYDAY LIVING *Janet Harris*	2.00
___ ASTROLOGY MADE EASY *Astarte*	3.00
___ ASTROLOGY MADE PRACTICAL *Alexandra Kayhle*	3.00
___ ASTROLOGY, ROMANCE, YOU AND THE STARS *Anthony Norvell*	4.00
___ MY WORLD OF ASTROLOGY *Sydney Omarr*	5.00
___ THOUGHT DIAL *Sidney Omarr*	4.00
___ WHAT THE STARS REVEAL ABOUT THE MEN IN YOUR LIFE *Thelma White*	3.00

BRIDGE

___ BRIDGE BIDDING MADE EASY *Edwin B. Kantar*	7.00
___ BRIDGE CONVENTIONS *Edwin B. Kantar*	7.00
___ BRIDGE HUMOR *Edwin B. Kantar*	5.00
___ COMPETITIVE BIDDING IN MODERN BRIDGE *Edgar Kaplan*	4.00
___ DEFENSIVE BRIDGE PLAY COMPLETE *Edwin B. Kantar*	10.00
___ GAMESMAN BRIDGE—Play Better with Kantar *Edwin B. Kantar*	5.00
___ HOW TO IMPROVE YOUR BRIDGE *Alfred Sheinwold*	5.00
___ IMPROVING YOUR BIDDING SKILLS *Edwin B. Kantar*	4.00
___ INTRODUCTION TO DECLARER'S PLAY *Edwin B. Kantar*	5.00
___ INTRODUCTION TO DEFENDER'S PLAY *Edwin B. Kantar*	3.00
___ KANTAR FOR THE DEFENSE *Edwin B. Kantar*	5.00
___ SHORT CUT TO WINNING BRIDGE *Alfred Sheinwold*	3.00
___ TEST YOUR BRIDGE PLAY *Edwin B. Kantar*	5.00
___ VOLUME 2—TEST YOUR BRIDGE PLAY *Edwin B. Kantar*	5.00
___ WINNING DECLARER PLAY *Dorothy Hayden Truscott*	4.00

BUSINESS, STUDY & REFERENCE

___ CONVERSATION MADE EASY *Elliot Russell*	3.00
___ EXAM SECRET *Dennis B. Jackson*	3.00
___ FIX-IT BOOK *Arthur Symons*	2.00
___ HOW TO DEVELOP A BETTER SPEAKING VOICE *M. Hellier*	3.00
___ HOW TO MAKE A FORTUNE IN REAL ESTATE *Albert Winnikoff*	4.00
___ INCREASE YOUR LEARNING POWER *Geoffrey A. Dudley*	3.00
___ MAGIC OF NUMBERS *Robert Tocquet*	2.00
___ PRACTICAL GUIDE TO BETTER CONCENTRATION *Melvin Powers*	3.00
___ PRACTICAL GUIDE TO PUBLIC SPEAKING *Maurice Forley*	5.00
___ 7 DAYS TO FASTER READING *William S. Schaill*	3.00
___ SONGWRITERS' RHYMING DICTIONARY *Jane Shaw Whitfield*	5.00
___ SPELLING MADE EASY *Lester D. Basch & Dr. Milton Finkelstein*	3.00
___ STUDENT'S GUIDE TO BETTER GRADES *J. A. Rickard*	3.00
___ TEST YOURSELF—Find Your Hidden Talent *Jack Shafer*	3.00
___ YOUR WILL & WHAT TO DO ABOUT IT *Attorney Samuel G. Kling*	4.00

CALLIGRAPHY

___ ADVANCED CALLIGRAPHY *Katherine Jeffares*	7.00
___ CALLIGRAPHER'S REFERENCE BOOK *Anne Leptich & Jacque Evans*	7.00
___ CALLIGRAPHY—The Art of Beautiful Writing *Katherine Jeffares*	7.00
___ CALLIGRAPHY FOR FUN & PROFIT *Anne Leptich & Jacque Evans*	7.00
___ CALLIGRAPHY MADE EASY *Tina Serafini*	7.00

CHESS & CHECKERS

___ BEGINNER'S GUIDE TO WINNING CHESS *Fred Reinfeld*	4.00
___ CHECKERS MADE EASY *Tom Wiswell*	2.00
___ CHESS IN TEN EASY LESSONS *Larry Evans*	3.00
___ CHESS MADE EASY *Milton L. Hanauer*	3.00
___ CHESS PROBLEMS FOR BEGINNERS *edited by Fred Reinfeld*	2.00
___ CHESS SECRETS REVEALED *Fred Reinfeld*	2.00
___ CHESS STRATEGY—An Expert's Guide *Fred Reinfeld*	2.00
___ CHESS TACTICS FOR BEGINNERS *edited by Fred Reinfeld*	3.00
___ CHESS THEORY & PRACTICE *Morry & Mitchell*	2.00
___ HOW TO WIN AT CHECKERS *Fred Reinfeld*	3.00
___ 1001 BRILLIANT WAYS TO CHECKMATE *Fred Reinfeld*	4.00

_____ 1001 WINNING CHESS SACRIFICES & COMBINATIONS *Fred Reinfeld*   4.

_____ SOVIET CHESS *Edited by R. G. Wade*   3.

COOKERY & HERBS

_____ CULPEPER'S HERBAL REMEDIES *Dr. Nicholas Culpeper*   3.

_____ FAST GOURMET COOKBOOK *Poppy Cannon*   2.

_____ GINSENG The Myth & The Truth *Joseph P. Hou*   3.

_____ HEALING POWER OF HERBS *May Bethel*   4.

_____ HEALING POWER OF NATURAL FOODS *May Bethel*   4.

_____ HERB HANDBOOK *Dawn MacLeod*   3.

_____ HERBS FOR COOKING AND HEALING *Dr. Donald Law*   3.

_____ HERBS FOR HEALTH—How to Grow & Use Them *Louise Evans Doole*   3.

_____ HOME GARDEN COOKBOOK—Delicious Natural Food Recipes *Ken Kraft*   3.

_____ MEDICAL HERBALIST *edited by Dr. J. R. Yemm*   3.

_____ NATURAL FOOD COOKBOOK *Dr. Harry C. Bond*   3.

_____ NATURE'S MEDICINES *Richard Lucas*   3.

_____ VEGETABLE GARDENING FOR BEGINNERS *Hugh Wiberg*   2.

_____ VEGETABLES FOR TODAY'S GARDENS *R. Milton Carleton*   2.

_____ VEGETARIAN COOKERY *Janet Walker*   4.

_____ VEGETARIAN COOKING MADE EASY & DELECTABLE *Veronica Vezza*   3.

_____ VEGETARIAN DELIGHTS—A Happy Cookbook for Health *K. R. Mehta*   2.

_____ VEGETARIAN GOURMET COOKBOOK *Joyce McKinnel*   3.

GAMBLING & POKER

_____ ADVANCED POKER STRATEGY & WINNING PLAY *A. D. Livingston*   5.

_____ HOW NOT TO LOSE AT POKER *Jeffrey Lloyd Castle*   3.

_____ HOW TO WIN AT DICE GAMES *Skip Frey*   3.

_____ HOW TO WIN AT POKER *Terence Reese & Anthony T. Watkins*   3.

_____ SECRETS OF WINNING POKER *George S. Coffin*   3.

_____ WINNING AT CRAPS *Dr. Lloyd T. Commins*   3.

_____ WINNING AT GIN *Chester Wander & Cy Rice*   3.

_____ WINNING AT POKER—An Expert's Guide *John Archer*   3.

_____ WINNING AT 21—An Expert's Guide *John Archer*   5.

_____ WINNING POKER SYSTEMS *Norman Zadeh*   3.

HEALTH

_____ BEE POLLEN *Lynda Lyngheim & Jack Scagnetti*   3.

_____ DR. LINDNER'S SPECIAL WEIGHT CONTROL METHOD *P. G. Lindner, M.D.*   2.

_____ HELP YOURSELF TO BETTER SIGHT *Margaret Darst Corbett*   3.

_____ HOW TO IMPROVE YOUR VISION *Dr. Robert A. Kraskin*   3.

_____ HOW YOU CAN STOP SMOKING PERMANENTLY *Ernest Caldwell*   3.

_____ MIND OVER PLATTER *Peter G. Lindner, M.D.*   3.

_____ NATURE'S WAY TO NUTRITION & VIBRANT HEALTH *Robert J. Scrutton*   3.

_____ NEW CARBOHYDRATE DIET COUNTER *Patti Lopez-Pereira*   1.

_____ QUICK & EASY EXERCISES FOR FACIAL BEAUTY *Judy Smith-deal*   2.

_____ QUICK & EASY EXERCISES FOR FIGURE BEAUTY *Judy Smith-deal*   2.

_____ REFLEXOLOGY *Dr. Maybelle Segal*   3.

_____ REFLEXOLOGY FOR GOOD HEALTH *Anna Kaye & Don C. Matchan*   3.

_____ YOU CAN LEARN TO RELAX *Dr. Samuel Gutwirth*   3.

_____ YOUR ALLERGY—What To Do About It *Allan Knight, M.D.*   3.

HOBBIES

_____ BEACHCOMBING FOR BEGINNERS *Norman Hickin*   2.

_____ BLACKSTONE'S MODERN CARD TRICKS *Harry Blackstone*   3.

_____ BLACKSTONE'S SECRETS OF MAGIC *Harry Blackstone*   3.

_____ COIN COLLECTING FOR BEGINNERS *Burton Hobson & Fred Reinfeld*   3.

_____ ENTERTAINING WITH ESP *Tony 'Doc' Shiels*   4.

_____ 400 FASCINATING MAGIC TRICKS YOU CAN DO *Howard Thurston*   4.

_____ HOW I TURN JUNK INTO FUN AND PROFIT *Sari*   3.

_____ HOW TO WRITE A HIT SONG & SELL IT *Tommy Boyce*   7.

_____ JUGGLING MADE EASY *Rudolf Dittrich*   2.

_____ MAGIC FOR ALL AGES *Walter Gibson*   4.

_____ MAGIC MADE EASY *Byron Wels*   2.

_____ STAMP COLLECTING FOR BEGINNERS *Burton Hobson*   3.

HORSE PLAYERS' WINNING GUIDES

_____ BETTING HORSES TO WIN *Les Conklin*   3.

_____ ELIMINATE THE LOSERS *Bob McKnight*   3.

__ HOW TO PICK WINNING HORSES *Bob McKnight*	3.00
__ HOW TO WIN AT THE RACES *Sam (The Genius) Lewin*	5.00
__ HOW YOU CAN BEAT THE RACES *Jack Kavanagh*	5.00
__ MAKING MONEY AT THE RACES *David Barr*	3.00
__ PAYDAY AT THE RACES *Les Conklin*	3.00
__ SMART HANDICAPPING MADE EASY *William Bauman*	3.00
__ SUCCESS AT THE HARNESS RACES *Barry Meadow*	3.00
__ WINNING AT THE HARNESS RACES—An Expert's Guide *Nick Cammarano*	3.00

HUMOR

__ HOW TO BE A COMEDIAN FOR FUN & PROFIT *King & Laufer*	2.00
__ HOW TO FLATTEN YOUR TUSH *Coach Marge Reardon*	2.00
__ HOW TO MAKE LOVE TO YOURSELF *Ron Stevens & Joy Grdnic*	3.00
__ JOKE TELLER'S HANDBOOK *Bob Orben*	3.00
__ JOKES FOR ALL OCCASIONS *Al Schock*	3.00
__ 2000 NEW LAUGHS FOR SPEAKERS *Bob Orben*	4.00
__ 2,500 JOKES TO START 'EM LAUGHING *Bob Orben*	4.00

HYPNOTISM

__ ADVANCED TECHNIQUES OF HYPNOSIS *Melvin Powers*	2.00
__ BRAINWASHING AND THE CULTS *Paul A. Verdier, Ph.D.*	3.00
__ CHILDBIRTH WITH HYPNOSIS *William S. Kroger, M.D.*	5.00
__ HOW TO SOLVE Your Sex Problems with Self-Hypnosis *Frank S. Caprio, M.D.*	5.00
__ HOW TO STOP SMOKING THRU SELF-HYPNOSIS *Leslie M. LeCron*	3.00
__ HOW TO USE AUTO-SUGGESTION EFFECTIVELY *John Duckworth*	3.00
__ HOW YOU CAN BOWL BETTER USING SELF-HYPNOSIS *Jack Heise*	3.00
__ HOW YOU CAN PLAY BETTER GOLF USING SELF-HYPNOSIS *Jack Heise*	3.00
__ HYPNOSIS AND SELF-HYPNOSIS *Bernard Hollander, M.D.*	3.00
__ HYPNOTISM *(Originally published in 1893) Carl Sextus*	5.00
__ HYPNOTISM & PSYCHIC PHENOMENA *Simeon Edmunds*	4.00
__ HYPNOTISM MADE EASY *Dr. Ralph Winn*	3.00
__ HYPNOTISM MADE PRACTICAL *Louis Orton*	3.00
__ HYPNOTISM REVEALED *Melvin Powers*	2.00
__ HYPNOTISM TODAY *Leslie LeCron and Jean Bordeaux, Ph.D.*	5.00
__ MODERN HYPNOSIS *Lesley Kuhn & Salvatore Russo, Ph.D.*	5.00
__ NEW CONCEPTS OF HYPNOSIS *Bernard C. Gindes, M.D.*	5.00
__ NEW SELF-HYPNOSIS *Paul Adams*	4.00
__ POST-HYPNOTIC INSTRUCTIONS—Suggestions for Therapy *Arnold Furst*	3.00
__ PRACTICAL GUIDE TO SELF-HYPNOSIS *Melvin Powers*	3.00
__ PRACTICAL HYPNOTISM *Philip Magonet, M.D.*	3.00
__ SECRETS OF HYPNOTISM *S. J. Van Pelt, M.D.*	5.00
__ SELF-HYPNOSIS A Conditioned-Response Technique *Laurence Sparks*	5.00
__ SELF-HYPNOSIS Its Theory, Technique & Application *Melvin Powers*	3.00
__ THERAPY THROUGH HYPNOSIS *edited by Raphael H. Rhodes*	4.00

JUDAICA

__ MODERN ISRAEL *Lily Edelman*	2.00
__ SERVICE OF THE HEART *Evelyn Garfiel, Ph.D.*	4.00
__ STORY OF ISRAEL IN COINS *Jean & Maurice Gould*	2.00
__ STORY OF ISRAEL IN STAMPS *Maxim & Gabriel Shamir*	1.00
__ TONGUE OF THE PROPHETS *Robert St. John*	5.00

JUST FOR WOMEN

__ COSMOPOLITAN'S GUIDE TO MARVELOUS MEN Fwd. by *Helen Gurley Brown*	3.00
__ COSMOPOLITAN'S HANG-UP HANDBOOK Foreword by *Helen Gurley Brown*	4.00
__ COSMOPOLITAN'S LOVE BOOK—A Guide to Ecstasy in Bed	4.00
__ COSMOPOLITAN'S NEW ETIQUETTE GUIDE Fwd. by *Helen Gurley Brown*	4.00
__ I AM A COMPLEAT WOMAN *Doris Hagopian & Karen O'Connor Sweeney*	3.00
__ JUST FOR WOMEN—A Guide to the Female Body *Richard E. Sand, M.D.*	5.00
__ NEW APPROACHES TO SEX IN MARRIAGE *John E. Eichenlaub, M.D.*	3.00
__ SEXUALLY ADEQUATE FEMALE *Frank S. Caprio, M.D.*	3.00
__ SEXUALLY FULFILLED WOMAN *Dr. Rachel Copelan*	5.00
__ YOUR FIRST YEAR OF MARRIAGE *Dr. Tom McGinnis*	3.00

MARRIAGE, SEX & PARENTHOOD

__ ABILITY TO LOVE *Dr. Allan Fromme*	5.00
__ ENCYCLOPEDIA OF MODERN SEX & LOVE TECHNIQUES *Macandrew*	5.00
__ GUIDE TO SUCCESSFUL MARRIAGE *Drs. Albert Ellis & Robert Harper*	5.00

_____ HOW TO RAISE AN EMOTIONALLY HEALTHY, HAPPY CHILD *A. Ellis*   4
_____ SEX WITHOUT GUILT *Albert Ellis, Ph.D.*   5
_____ SEXUALLY ADEQUATE MALE *Frank S. Caprio, M.D.*   3
_____ SEXUALLY FULFILLED MAN *Dr. Rachel Copelan*   5

MELVIN POWERS' MAIL ORDER LIBRARY

_____ HOW TO GET RICH IN MAIL ORDER *Melvin Powers*   10
_____ HOW TO WRITE A GOOD ADVERTISEMENT *Victor O. Schwab*   15
_____ MAIL ORDER MADE EASY *J. Frank Brumbaugh*   10
_____ U.S. MAIL ORDER SHOPPER'S GUIDE *Susan Spitzer*   10

METAPHYSICS & OCCULT

_____ BOOK OF TALISMANS, AMULETS & ZODIACAL GEMS *William Pavitt*   5
_____ CONCENTRATION—A Guide to Mental Mastery *Mouni Sadhu*
_____ CRITIQUES OF GOD *Edited by Peter Angeles*
_____ EXTRA-TERRESTRIAL INTELLIGENCE—The First Encounter
_____ FORTUNE TELLING WITH CARDS *P. Foli*
_____ HANDWRITING ANALYSIS MADE EASY *John Marley*
_____ HANDWRITING TELLS *Nadya Olyanova*
_____ HOW TO INTERPRET DREAMS, OMENS & FORTUNE TELLING SIGNS *Gettings*
_____ HOW TO UNDERSTAND YOUR DREAMS *Geoffrey A. Dudley*
_____ ILLUSTRATED YOGA *William Zorn*
_____ IN DAYS OF GREAT PEACE *Mouni Sadhu*
_____ LSD—THE AGE OF MIND *Bernard Roseman*
_____ MAGICIAN—His Training and Work *W. E. Butler*
_____ MEDITATION *Mouni Sadhu*
_____ MODERN NUMEROLOGY *Morris C. Goodman*
_____ NUMEROLOGY—ITS FACTS AND SECRETS *Ariel Yvon Taylor*
_____ NUMEROLOGY MADE EASY *W. Mykian*
_____ PALMISTRY MADE EASY *Fred Gettings*
_____ PALMISTRY MADE PRACTICAL *Elizabeth Daniels Squire*
_____ PALMISTRY SECRETS REVEALED *Henry Frith*
_____ PROPHECY IN OUR TIME *Martin Ebon*
_____ PSYCHOLOGY OF HANDWRITING *Nadya Olyanova*
_____ SUPERSTITION—Are You Superstitious? *Eric Maple*
_____ TAROT *Mouni Sadhu*
_____ TAROT OF THE BOHEMIANS *Papus*
_____ WAYS TO SELF-REALIZATION *Mouni Sadhu*
_____ WHAT YOUR HANDWRITING REVEALS *Albert E. Hughes*
_____ WITCHCRAFT, MAGIC & OCCULTISM—A Fascinating History *W. B. Crow*
_____ WITCHCRAFT—THE SIXTH SENSE *Justine Glass*
_____ WORLD OF PSYCHIC RESEARCH *Hereward Carrington*

SELF-HELP & INSPIRATIONAL

_____ DAILY POWER FOR JOYFUL LIVING *Dr. Donald Curtis*
_____ DYNAMIC THINKING *Melvin Powers*
_____ EXUBERANCE—Your Guide to Happiness & Fulfillment *Dr. Paul Kurtz*
_____ GREATEST POWER IN THE UNIVERSE *U. S. Andersen*
_____ GROW RICH WHILE YOU SLEEP *Ben Sweetland*
_____ GROWTH THROUGH REASON *Albert Ellis, Ph.D.*
_____ GUIDE TO DEVELOPING YOUR POTENTIAL *Herbert A. Otto, Ph.D.*
_____ GUIDE TO LIVING IN BALANCE *Frank S. Caprio, M.D.*
_____ GUIDE TO PERSONAL HAPPINESS *Albert Ellis, Ph.D. & Irving Becker, Ed. D.*
_____ HELPING YOURSELF WITH APPLIED PSYCHOLOGY *R. Henderson*
_____ HELPING YOURSELF WITH PSYCHIATRY *Frank S. Caprio, M.D.*
_____ HOW TO ATTRACT GOOD LUCK *A. H. Z. Carr*
_____ HOW TO CONTROL YOUR DESTINY *Norvell*
_____ HOW TO DEVELOP A WINNING PERSONALITY *Martin Panzer*
_____ HOW TO DEVELOP AN EXCEPTIONAL MEMORY *Young & Gibson*
_____ HOW TO LIVE WITH A NEUROTIC *Albert Ellis, Ph. D.*
_____ HOW TO OVERCOME YOUR FEARS *M. P. Leahy, M.D.*
_____ HOW YOU CAN HAVE CONFIDENCE AND POWER *Les Giblin*
_____ HUMAN PROBLEMS & HOW TO SOLVE THEM *Dr. Donald Curtis*
_____ I CAN *Ben Sweetland*
_____ I WILL *Ben Sweetland*
_____ LEFT-HANDED PEOPLE *Michael Barsley*

___ MAGIC IN YOUR MIND *U. S. Andersen*   5.00
___ MAGIC OF THINKING BIG *Dr. David J. Schwartz*   3.00
___ MAGIC POWER OF YOUR MIND *Walter M. Germain*   5.00
___ MENTAL POWER THROUGH SLEEP SUGGESTION *Melvin Powers*   3.00
___ NEW GUIDE TO RATIONAL LIVING *Albert Ellis, Ph.D. & R. Harper, Ph.D.*   3.00
___ OUR TROUBLED SELVES *Dr. Allan Fromme*   3.00
___ PSYCHO-CYBERNETICS *Maxwell Maltz, M.D.*   3.00
___ SCIENCE OF MIND IN DAILY LIVING *Dr. Donald Curtis*   5.00
___ SECRET OF SECRETS *U. S. Andersen*   5.00
___ SECRET POWER OF THE PYRAMIDS *U. S. Andersen*   5.00
___ STUTTERING AND WHAT YOU CAN DO ABOUT IT *W. Johnson, Ph.D.*   2.50
___ SUCCESS-CYBERNETICS *U. S. Andersen*   5.00
___ 10 DAYS TO A GREAT NEW LIFE *William E. Edwards*   3.00
___ THINK AND GROW RICH *Napoleon Hill*   3.00
___ THINK YOUR WAY TO SUCCESS *Dr. Lew Losoncy*   5.00
___ THREE MAGIC WORDS *U. S. Andersen*   5.00
___ TREASURY OF COMFORT *edited by Rabbi Sidney Greenberg*   5.00
___ TREASURY OF THE ART OF LIVING *Sidney S. Greenberg*   5.00
___ YOU ARE NOT THE TARGET *Laura Huxley*   5.00
___ YOUR SUBCONSCIOUS POWER *Charles M. Simmons*   5.00
___ YOUR THOUGHTS CAN CHANGE YOUR LIFE *Dr. Donald Curtis*   5.00

SPORTS

___ BICYCLING FOR FUN AND GOOD HEALTH *Kenneth E. Luther*   2.00
___ BILLIARDS—Pocket • Carom • Three Cushion *Clive Cottingham, Jr.*   3.00
___ CAMPING-OUT 101 Ideas & Activities *Bruno Knobel*   2.00
___ COMPLETE GUIDE TO FISHING *Vlad Evanoff*   2.00
___ HOW TO IMPROVE YOUR RACQUETBALL *Lubarsky Kaufman & Scagnetti*   3.00
___ HOW TO WIN AT POCKET BILLIARDS *Edward D. Knuchell*   4.00
___ JOY OF WALKING *Jack Scagnetti*   3.00
___ LEARNING & TEACHING SOCCER SKILLS *Eric Worthington*   3.00
___ MOTORCYCLING FOR BEGINNERS *I. G. Edmonds*   3.00
___ RACQUETBALL FOR WOMEN *Toni Hudson, Jack Scagnetti & Vince Rondone*   3.00
___ RACQUETBALL MADE EASY *Steve Lubarsky, Rod Delson & Jack Scagnetti*   4.00
___ SECRET OF BOWLING STRIKES *Dawson Taylor*   3.00
___ SECRET OF PERFECT PUTTING *Horton Smith & Dawson Taylor*   3.00
___ SOCCER—The Game & How to Play It *Gary Rosenthal*   3.00
___ STARTING SOCCER *Edward F. Dolan, Jr.*   3.00
___ TABLE TENNIS MADE EASY *Johnny Leach*   2.00

TENNIS LOVERS' LIBRARY

___ BEGINNER'S BUIDE TO WINNING TENNIS *Helen Hull Jacobs*   2.00
___ HOW TO BEAT BETTER TENNIS PLAYERS *Loring Fiske*   4.00
___ HOW TO IMPROVE YOUR TENNIS—Style, Strategy & Analysis *C. Wilson*   2.00
___ INSIDE TENNIS—Techniques of Winning *Jim Leighton*   3.00
___ PLAY TENNIS WITH ROSEWALL *Ken Rosewall*   2.00
___ PSYCH YOURSELF TO BETTER TENNIS *Dr. Walter A. Luszki*   2.00
___ SUCCESSFUL TENNIS *Neale Fraser*   2.00
___ TENNIS FOR BEGINNERS, *Dr. H. A. Murray*   2.00
___ TENNIS MADE EASY *Joel Brecheen*   3.00
___ WEEKEND TENNIS—How to Have Fun & Win at the Same Time *Bill Talbert*   3.00
___ WINNING WITH PERCENTAGE TENNIS—Smart Strategy *Jack Lowe*   2.00

WILSHIRE PET LIBRARY

___ DOG OBEDIENCE TRAINING *Gust Kessopulos*   5.00
___ DOG TRAINING MADE EASY & FUN *John W. Kellogg*   4.00
___ HOW TO BRING UP YOUR PET DOG *Kurt Unkelbach*   2.00
___ HOW TO RAISE & TRAIN YOUR PUPPY *Jeff Griffen*   3.00
___ PIGEONS: HOW TO RAISE & TRAIN THEM *William H. Allen, Jr.*   2.00

The books listed above can be obtained from your book dealer or directly from Melvin Powers. When ordering, please remit 50¢ per book postage & handling. Send for our free illustrated catalog of self-improvement books.

Melvin Powers

12015 Sherman Road, No. Hollywood, California 91605

Notes

Notes

Notes

Notes

Notes

Notes

Notes